THE PRINCETON REVIEW

Alternative Careers
for Lawyers

THE PRINCETON REVIEW

Alternative Careers for Lawyers

By Hillary Mantis

Random House, Inc.
New York, 1997
http://www.randomhouse.com

Princeton Review Publishing, L.L.C.
2315 Broadway
New York, NY 10024
E-mail: info@review.com

ISBN 0-679-77870-5

Editor: Amy Zavatto
Designer: Illeny Maaza
Production Editor: Bruno Blumenfeld

Manufactured in the United States of America on partially recycled paper.

9 8 7 6 5 4 3 2 1

First Edition

DEDICATION

To—Jenna, Spencer, Andy and Linda, and Trudy and Art (in no particular order!)

ACKNOWLEDGMENTS

I wish to thank my research assistant, Michael Arseneault— without his help and tremendous research skills, this book could not have been completed. I would also like to express my appreciation for the people at Fordham who made this (and many other things in my professional life) possible, especially Assistant Dean Kathleen Brady and Dean John Feerick.

Many thanks as well to Amy Zavatto, my editor, who guided me through this project with much encouragement and enthusiasm.

TABLE OF CONTENTS

Acknowledgments   v

Preface   ix

Chapter 1   **Thinking About Leaving**   1

Chapter 2   **Salary Considerations**   11

Chapter 3   **Transitional Strategies**   29

Chapter 4   **Making It Happen: Initial Steps Out**   71

Chapter 5   **Women Lawyers: A Special Case**   89

Chapter 6   **Profiles**   99

Chapter 7   **Sample Resumes**   139

Chapter 8   **Non-Practicing Famous Lawyers**   151

Chapter 9   **Resources**   155

                     Appendix   159

About the Author   173

Preface

So you got your J.D. after years of hard work, and guess what? You're not happy. What should you do now? You can take a deep breath and leave the profession entirely. Or you can stay and suffer. But perhaps there's another way. Perhaps there is a way to either stay, and be content, or to leave, and not feel guilty or defensive. Maybe there is even a way to leave and to *still* make money.

By the time you finish reading this book, you will know what to do. You will have the opportunity to read "true-life" stories of lawyers who have successfully transitioned into many other successful and rewarding fields. One of them is rich beyond her wildest dreams. One has her own company, leading bicycle tours around the world. Another is a television commentator. Still another has made peace with the profession by helping other lawyers make career transitions.

Reading their stories will help you decide what to do, and more importantly show you how possible it is to find career satisfaction. After you read the profiles, you will learn everything there is to know about moving into your targeted career. You will learn how to take your resume and rewrite it so it can be used for another profession. You will learn to write convincing cover letters, master difficult interviewing situations, and use your legal skills to negotiate yourself a fair salary. You will also learn how to take a sabbatical, if you need a break....But most of all, you will no longer be miserable!

As Robert Frost said, "I took the road less traveled by, and it made all of the difference."

Thinking About Leaving

According to a 1992 poll conducted by *California Lawyer* magazine, 70 percent of lawyers surveyed said they would start a new career if they could. A 1990 American Bar Association survey indicated that 23 percent of all lawyers were dissatisfied with their careers. A 1990 Johns Hopkins University study found that lawyers had a greater rate of depression than workers in any of the 104 other occupations studied.

An anonymous California lawyer and journalist (whose nom de plume is "The Rodent") writes a column about life as an associate inside of America's law firms. The Rodent receives many letters from other lawyers. "Many of us feel trapped...and can relate to the frustration and other emotions expressed by the lawyers who wrote these letters," concludes a recent column. An associate from Florida sums up his existence this way: "Wake up in the morning, bill, eat, bill, eat and bill at the same time, bill, go to sleep."

Other lawyers have referred to themselves as "slaves" or "gerbils" in their anonymous letters.

Could things get worse? Well, yes. Lawyers have among the highest suicide rates, lowest popularity ratings, highest pressure, and longest hours of almost any profession that exists. It's depressing, to say the least. On top of that, since 1989 lawyers have been subject to the previously unheard of sting of layoffs and downsizing.

For those of us who grew up watching lawyers in film and television, it *seemed* like it would be an interesting profession. *Anatomy of a Murder*, *12 Angry Men*, *To Kill a Mockingbird*, and *The Caine Mutiny*, all classics, portrayed lawyers who made a difference. More recently, television programs such as "L.A. Law" made the profession seem lucrative and glamorous, if not honorable. Even the O.J. Simpson trial showed lawyers involved in high drama and theatrics analogous to the best Perry Mason episodes.

Who knew that the real-life young lawyers of the 1980s and 1990s would be writing anonymous letters to an unhappy associate named The Rodent proclaiming themselves "slaves(s)...working in vile litigation sweatshops."

This feeling is not limited to young lawyers alone. The majority of calls that Richard Carleton, head of a California-based program for lawyers, receives are from solo practitioners and associates in small group practices. Many of these lawyers have financial struggles on top of all of their work pressures.

It's not much better for partners these days either. In an *American Lawyer* article entitled "Misery," a successful partner at Covington and Burling, and former president of Harvard Law School's Alumni Association, said, "If any of my children ends up going into the practice of law, I will consider myself to have been defeated." Even among the partners at the most prestigious firms, there is dissatisfaction. In recent years, the security of being a partner has ebbed as well, and brutal competition for clients now equals brutal competition for the most billable hours.

WHY ARE LAWYERS SO UNHAPPY?

Perhaps the most comprehensive study of lawyer dissatisfaction was conducted by the American Bar Association Young Lawyer's Division in 1990. The 3,000-plus "young lawyers" (defined as under age 36 or less than three years in practice) interviewed cited three major problems causing job dissatisfaction:

1. Lack of time for self and family, due to billable hours requirement.

2. Failure to communicate and isolation within the firm.

3. <u>Lack of training or mentoring within the firm</u>.

Ten Major Factors for Lawyer Unhappiness:

1. Lack of control
2. Poor quality of life
3. Expectations did not meet reality
4. Adversarial nature of practice
5. Extreme pressure/overwork
6. Wrong career choice
7. <u>No sense of personal satisfaction from wor</u>k
8. Wrong choice of practice setting/area of practice
9. Less job security than anticipated
10. Work tedious; not as interesting as expected

(Source: *The New York Times*, May 21, 1996)

According to Assistant Dean Kathleen Brady of Fordham University Law School, "Expectations fail to meet reality when law students graduate and enter the work force." In recent years, law students are deciding to seek alternatives before graduating from law school. Fordham's Class of 1995, like other schools, indicated an increase (to about seven percent of the class) in the number of its graduates pursuing non-legal careers upon graduation. "Beginning in law school, many law students blindly aspire to be partners rather than lawyers. ...Yet despite these disenchanted lawyers' focus upon 'partnership' status, surprisingly, most are incredibly naive about law as a business....Thankfully the trend seems to be shifting," (according to one attorney participating in an online comment discussion about the legal profession).

Survival Tips For Associates:

- Negotiate flexible hours
- Do something to alleviate the pressure
- Accept that there will be some tedium
- Increase your job satisfaction
- Take charge
- Become a "Producer": Develop rainmaking skills that will enable you to bring in new clients and business
- Find a mentor to help you navigate office politics
- Ask for feedback
- Have your own set of goals: Develop a five-year plan for what you want to accomplish
- Be proactive: Ask questions when you are confused, suggest a training program if it does not exist, take advantage of programs that are offered, read the news to see where the next "hot practice area" might emerge
- Learn how to negotiate (See chapter 4)

This sense of disenchantment continues as lawyers advance into the profession. A recent online exchange on American Lawyer's Counsel Connect involved a group of lawyers mulling over the state of the profession. Among the reasons given for professional dissatisfaction were that the profession "requires lawyers to take responsibility for outcomes they cannot control..., [we are] involved in procedures that don't tend to resolve disputes or make the world a better place." Another participant commented, "Lawyers I have met don't like being lawyers... [they] feel that way because they are tired of the pressure, their everyday tasks are boring, and their accomplishments are not fulfilling. Remember that these are intelligent, well-educated, and often creative people who have found that the law was not all it was cracked up to be."

In the profiles of lawyers interviewed for this book, the most common threads of job unhappiness relate to a lack of guidance, lack of mentors, lack of fulfillment with their work, disappointment with the realities of how much they could earn, lack of appropriate treatment by senior associates, and pure burnout, caused by overwork. Their comments echo those cited by the major studies of lawyer career dissatisfaction: "The long hours, the pressure to make partner...the responsibility of telling people the correct answer...If I miss something there is a tremendous cost to being wrong," said one former attorney.

As you advance, you are the responsible party, sometimes with life-or-death responsibility on your shoulders. "The law is too insulated, too far removed. And the reward for doing a good job is more work and more pressure," according to human resources expert Jo Casey.

In my own experience counseling students and lawyers over the years, I have noticed that, ironically, it is the students who graduate with the most highly coveted jobs—associates at large law firms—who are the most unhappy lawyers. The same students who were envied by their law school peers often would call me, furtively, with the door closed and whisper about how desperate they felt. Life as an associate in a large firm is by almost all accounts, highly stressful and at times tedious.

In addition, the law is the only profession with an "up-or-out" system. Even if you are the best and the brightest, which young associates often are, there is no guarantee of making partner, and if you don't you eventually have to leave the firm. The volatile economy of law firms of the 1990s has further contributed to the associate's sense of fear, instability, extreme competition, and depression.

Factors Important to Lawyer Satisfaction:

- Intellectual stimulation and satisfaction
- Flexible work schedules
- Personal relationships with clients
- Utilization of technology (laptops, modems, fax machines, cellular phones, and E-mail) to both increase efficiency and give them more time outside of the office
- Getting away from the billable hour (by working in government, teaching, or other areas where they are not required)
- Training, mentor programs, and feedback
- Money, social status
- Predictable working hours
- Time for family/personal life outside of work
- Opportunity to do pro bono Work
- Good support staff assistance

WHO ARE THE HAPPIEST LAWYERS?

If associates are potentially the unhappiest lawyers, especially those at large firms, then who are the happiest lawyers? *Are* there any happy lawyers?

The answer is yes: Among the most content lawyers are solo practitioners, public interest lawyers, law professors, and the new breed of contract and temporary lawyers. Peter Erlinder, the President of the National Lawyers Guild, an organization of public interest lawyers, is genuinely happy: "Public interest law gives people an opportunity to make an impact on the world and feel they are doing something of value." Thomas Schoenherr, Director of Fordham University's Public Interest Resource Center, agrees: "Although it's not a bed of wine and roses, in general, public interest lawyers seem happier." Public interest lawyers, although at the low end of the pay scale, reap immense personal satisfaction from their work. "I will do this for as long as I can afford to," said one young assistant district attorney in the sex crimes unit.

Of partners in private practice who like their work, most derive similar personal satisfaction. According to one, "I like practicing law... Sometimes I really *help people*." Another partner comments, "While I am occasionally unenthusiastic about practice, there are times I feel I have truly helped my clients." It is this old-fashioned, personal, traditional lawyer-client relationship that gave lawyers the title "counselor"—and it is a title that they value.

In large firms, the happiest lawyers seem to be those in "sexy" practice areas, such as entertainment law, or mergers and acquisitions. In recent years, large firm lawyers who embrace and enjoy their "rainmaking" (attracting new clients) duties, as well as their paper work, have likewise thrived.

We have also witnessed the re-emergence of solo practice as an attractive alternative to firm practice. People seem willing to give up money and status to gain a feeling of *control* over their lives. Solo practitioners do not have to answer to anyone but themselves and their clients. They control their time and their caseload. "I left large-firm practice for small/solo practice...and I can't imagine being desperate enough to return to a large firm," said one anonymous attorney. Computer technology has also been instrumental in making solo practice affordable.

Teaching law gives lawyers an opportunity both to be creative and to help people, leading to very high career satisfaction. Plus, the money's not bad.

**Risk of Leaving/
Risk of Staying**

Risk of Leaving:
• <u>Earn less money</u>
• <u>Lose prestige and status
  accorded to lawyers</u>

Risk of Staying (you may not have thought about this side of the equation!):
• Burnout, stress, fatigue
• Poor health (both physical and mental)
• Problems with marriage and family relationships
• <u>Never finding out what
  you love to do, both at
  work, and outside of
  work</u>

Finally, contract and temporary lawyering, a new but growing trend, allows lawyers to still earn a good salary, but have breaks in between assignments.

Are You In the Wrong Career, or Just the Wrong Job?

Well, to begin with, you concur with some, if not all, of the reasons cited for lawyer dissatisfaction. In fact, "dissatisfied" might even be a very nice way to describe how you feel about practicing law. So what do you do now? Before reading on about the wonderful world of ex-lawyers, you should first consider the source of your dissatisfaction. It is probably easier to shift gears, and see how that feels, than it is to abandon ship completely, only to discover it was not "the law," but the setting in which you were practicing.

Possible Solutions

Many people discover job satisfaction by switching from the private to the public sector, or vice-versa. Or from a large firm to a small firm. Sometimes where you are working is just not a good fit, or there may be political reasons why you cannot succeed. Often, the pressure of practicing in a large metropolitan area overwhelms any positive feelings you may have about practice. Try to differentiate the part of you that hates your "job" from the part of you that hates (or maybe actually likes) your profession.

The self-assessment exercises in chapter 4 may help you with this part of the process. Speaking with a career counselor, your peers, or even a therapist, or taking a short sabbatical (see chapter 6) may also help you gain some perspective to make a final decision. Remember that most decisions are not irrevocable—<u>you can always go back to being a lawyer...*if* you decide you want to</u>.

Can This Situation Be Improved?

There may also be steps you can take *within* your current job that will ease your current situation and, inevitably, your life.

Perhaps there is a way for you to gain greater control over your work. Technological advances may give you some bargaining power over how much time you have to spend in the office (face time). Laptop computers and modems have made the practice of law much more portable.

In addition, pro bono work or a volunteer activity outside of work may give you a greater sense of control over your life. Do something that fulfills you. Something you enjoy. Do things to gain perspective, like get away from your peers for a few hours a day.

Perhaps you should consider becoming a solo, temporary lawyer, or contract lawyer. Ironically, there are many more options for attorneys now that the economy is not as strong. Many more options/titles have been created.

Also, don't forget about resources that are right under your nose. Talk to others; don't isolate yourself. Join online conversations on the Internet or Counsel connect. If you want to remain anonymous, use a different name. But however you do it, vent! Take control of your health and mental well-being. Consider moving to a smaller city, or one highly rated for its lifestyle. One caveat: Some states require that you take their Bar Exam before you are allowed to practice in that state, while others will just allow you to waive in if you are in good standing (i.e., *Money* magazine in 1996 rated Madison, Wisconsin as the best city to live in). Do anything you can to improve your quality of life. Bill, a Fordham Law School alum, went to work at an 80-hour-a-week job at a high-profile Manhattan law firm. Within two years, he realized he was miserable. Not only did he have zero personal life, but when he did have free time there weren't the sort of outdoor activities available that didn't require a long drive up-state. What was his solution? Relocation. Bill had already taken and passed the Colorado Bar, and, since cold-weather sports were his all-time favorite, found a suitable position at a Denver law firm in the middle of ski country.

Is Leaving Worth the Risk?

After reading all of the above, balance the pros and cons and decide for yourself. Let the rest of the book help you to decide. See how you feel when you are reading it. Are you ready to leave, or do you have very mixed emotions? Do you want to try a reconciliation, or are you done with law for good? Trust your gut feelings and follow your instincts.

Salary Considerations

CHARTING YOUR FINANCIAL NEEDS

For most attorneys considering leaving the profession, the burning question is this: How much will you earn in a career outside of law? According to a 1995 Labor Department study of 65,000 households reported in *The New York Times* (5/14/95), lawyers are the highest paid workers in America today. With the exception of top corporate executives, lawyers are paid, on average, more than any other professionals, including doctors. (With the advent of managed health care, pay increases for doctors have slowed considerably.)

So, statistically speaking, leaving the law means that you will probably earn less money. However, there is such a disparity between large law firm salaries, which are very high, and most small law firm salaries, which are more on par with other professions, that unless you are with a large law firm in a major metropolitan area, leaving law might not result in a huge pay decrease for everyone. And, the majority of lawyers practicing in the United States are solo practitioners or in small law firms. In fact, of the 78 percent of lawyers in private practice, 23 percent are solo practitioners, and another 33 percent are in firms of fewer than ten attorneys (according to the A.B.A. State of the Legal Profession Study, 1990).

This trend has continued throughout the 1990s. In fact, only 12.5 percent of the class of 1995 law grads got jobs at firms employing 101 or more attorneys, according to the National Association for Law Placement. That leaves over 85 percent of recent law graduates nationwide at mid-sized or smaller firms, government agencies, or public interest jobs where the salaries are substantially lower.

While the 101+ size firms paid up to $85,000 for entry level attorneys (in New York City), the median salary for the rest of the graduating class nationwide was approximately $56,000, with a low of $25,000.

In addition, when you add up billable hours and a typical sixty-plus-hour workweek, you may not be earning as much as you think. In the chart below, you can see for yourself how salaries within the law vary tremendously:

TYPICAL LEGAL SALARY STRUCTURE

The following are the results of a nationwide survey of salaries in private law firms:

First-Year Associate:

Median: $56,000   Low: $25,000   High: $85,000

Seventh-Year Associate:

Median: $80,000   Low: $40,000   High: $198,000

(Source: National Association for Law Placement 1995-96 Associate Salary Survey, Annual Report on Compensation, as of 10/15/95).

MEDIAN BASE ASSOCIATE SALARIES BY SIZE OF FIRM

Associate Year	All Sizes	2-25	26-50	51-100	101-250	250+
First	$56,000	45,000	50,000	58,500	60,000	67,000
Second	$59,750	49,750	52,000	59,625	61,500	70,000
Third	$62,000	50,910	55,000	62,000	65,000	73,000
Fourth	$66,000	57,300	58,000	66,500	68,000	77,000
Fifth	$69,625	60,000	63,500	71,000	70,600	81,500
Sixth	$75,000	67,000	66,000	72,250	75,000	87,250
Seventh	$80,000	71,500	71,250	79,000	79,500	92,500
Eighth	$84,625	72,800	75,750	84,376	83,000	96,500

(Source: National Association for Law Placement)

BUDGET AND LIFESTYLE CONSIDERATIONS

Just because you can't afford a $30,000 a year job, doesn't mean you need to earn $300,000 to survive. You may be able to survive quite nicely on something in between. Spend some time figuring out a budget. Figure out what you would be willing to give for more free time, or a passion for your work. Seeing it all logically spelled out can help you make progress toward a decision.

Many lawyers also suffer from the "golden handcuffs" syndrome. They have locked themselves into a certain lifestyle and feel that they are unable to give it up. After they have changed careers, however, they realize that it was more a case of perspective than actual financial need. Focus on what you may be receiving in your new life that you really want, rather than what you might be giving up. Also realize that you are likely to earn as much or more than you did as a lawyer eventually, once you progress in your new career. The following monthly budget evaluation might help you unlock the proverbial golden handcuffs.

Outgoing (Bills/Expenses)

Rent/Mortgage: _____

Insurance Payments: _____

Phone Bill: _____

Cable: _____

Electric: _____

Heat: _____

Transportation: _____

Food: _____

Medical: _____

Household Expenses: _____

Credit Cards: _____

Child Care: _____

Clothing: _____

Student Loans: _____

Other Loans: _____

Other Expenses: _____

Incoming (Cash Flow)

Paycheck: _____

Investment Interest/Dividends: _____

Other Sources of Income
(consulting/freelance work, etc.):_____

Bonuses: _____

Your Assets

Home Ownership: _____

Automobiles: _____

Stocks, Bonds, Mutual Funds,
Other Investment Instruments: _____

Retirement Fund: _____

Art, Antiques, Jewelry, Other Collectibles: _____

Other: _____

After you have filled out the chart, distinguish the areas in
which you have some financial flexibility. What would you be
willing to give up for happiness, possibly shorter hours, and a
better lifestyle?

Now that you have information about what lawyers earn
and where your own earnings go, you can look at the average
standard of living in other professions that might interest you.

NONLEGAL CAREERS SALARY OVERVIEW

Profession	Initial Pay	Typical	Top Pay
Accounting & Finance			
Big Six firm	$ 30,125	$ 38,625	$ 69,750
Small firm	$ 24,750	$ 36,500	$ 63,000
Associate accountant	$ 25,000	$ 28,400	$ 31,200
Senior auditor	$ 37,200	$ 42,500	$ 48,600
Senior tax accountant	$ 46,900	$ 55,300	$ 62,800
Controller	$ 97,900	$147,900	$176,000
Treasurer	$108,000	$160,500	$191,100
CFO	$165,000	$277,200	$345,000
Advertising			
Advertising copywriter	$ 30,000	$ 50,000	$ 90,000
Art director	$ 27,500	$ 47,500	$ 82,500
Account executive	$ 28,000	$ 62,500	$375,000
Creative director	$150,000	$300,000	$500,000

Profession	Initial pay	Typical	Top Pay
Architecture			
Architect	$ 27,000	$ 35,000	$ 43,900
Principal/Partner	$ 35,000	$ 50,000	$110,000
CEO	$1,131,042	$1,524,057	$2,043,294
Consulting			
Strategic consultant	$ 47,677	$120,660	$307,667
Human resources			
consultant	$ 38,633	$ 64,218	$139,099
MIS consultant	$ 39,120	$ 81,569	$130,156
Corporate ethics			
Ethics administrator	$ 35,000	$ 50,000	$ 70,000
VP for ethics	$ 95,000	$140,000	$200,000
Education			
University professor	$ 39,050	$ 49,490	$ 63,450
Elementary teacher	$ 25,693	$ 36,357	$ 50,600
Secondary teacher	$ 26,077	$ 37,764	$ 53,300
Engineering			
Biomedical engineer	$ 37,750	$ 72,500	$150,000
Chemical engineer	$ 39,863	$ 73,970	$179,700
Civil engineer	$ 30,690	$ 62,000	$141,260
Electrical engineer	$ 33,000	$ 65,876	$146,000
Mechanical engineer	$ 36,935	$ 65,160	$155,734
Industrial engineer	$ 35,244	$ 67,000	$ 215,000
Financial services			
Financial planner	$ 27,000	$ 50,000	$200,000
Portfolio manager	$ 40,000	$100,000	$150,000
Loan officer			
Mortgage	$ 27,200	$ 54,600	$ 67,800
Commercial	$ 41,500	$ 71,000	$ 86,200
Actuary	$ 25,382	$ 36,914	$ 58,432
Insurance			
Life insurance			
underwriter	$ 23,500	$ 37,564	$ 52,563
Group insurance			
underwriter	$ 27,421	$ 38,883	$ 56,400
Government jobs			
Economist	$ 21,486	$ 46,852	$102,338
Budget analyst	$ 21,486	$ 38,885	$102,338
Personnel manager	$ 18,956	$ 46,852	$102,338
Agency head	—	—	$148,400

Profession	Initial pay	Typical	Top Pay
CIA director	—	—	$133,600
Congressman	—	—	$133,600
Cabinet member	—	—	$148,400
Health care			
Private	$ 86,300	$123,700	$169,400
HMO	$ 96,700	$123,300	$170,000
Neurosurgeon	$158,500	$263,300	$450,400
Cardiothoracic surgeon	$175,900	$312,300	$435,650
Plastic surgeon	$157,500	$181,000	$341,200
Registered nurse	$ 34,600	$ 39,800	$ 45,700
Licensed physical therapist	$ 35,500	$ 45,400	$ 53,800
High technology			
Software engineer	$ 33,702	$ 54,470	$ 75,524
Hardware engineer	$ 33,592	$ 54,704	$ 75,360
CD-ROM producer	$ 35,000	$ 60,000	$100,000
Human resources			
Employee-training manager	$ 49,500	$ 59,000	$ 65,700
Benefits manager	$ 63,800	$ 85,200	$101,600
Human resources VP	$118,100	$188,700	$235,600
Information services			
Programming trainee	$ 9,000	$ 19,500	$ 28,000
LAN/WAN specialist	$ 27,900	$ 41,000	$ 49,983
Database specialist	$ 33,228	$ 45,193	$ 69,000
Systems analyst	$ 35,728	$ 44,026	$ 49,270
Applications programmer	$ 25,992	$ 49,000	$ 55,000
MIS director	$ 57,700	$ 89,000	$210,000
IRS agent			
Tax auditor	$ 19,500	$ 34,000	$ 38,500
Revenue officer	$ 19,500	$ 34,000	$ 66,606
Revenue agent	$ 19,500	$ 49,663	$ 81,013
Investment banking			
Generalist	$ 95,000	$440,000	$ 1,250,000
M&A specialist	$ 95,000	$590,000	$ 1,750,000
Trader			
General instruments	$ 60,000	$290,000	$1,000,000
Foreign exchange or derivatives specialist	$ 60,000	$360,000	$2,000,000
Risk manager	$450,000	$725,000	$1,000,000
Retail stockbroker	$ 50,000	$150,000	$620,000
Institutional stockbroker	$ 88,000	$345,000	$ 1,000,000

Profession	Initial pay	Typical	Top Pay
Law			
Associate	$ 58,942	$ 74,318	$103,562
Partner	$114,213	$183,364	$301,611
Public prosecutor	$ 23,000	$ 30,000	$ 38,000
Public defender	$ 20,000	$ 28,900	$ 40,000
Corporate lawyer	$ 61,932	$ 79,297	$111,708
Chief legal officer	$169,300	$258,966	$445,000
Paralegal	$ 30,470	$ 37,686	$ 50,544
Lobbying			
Small trade group	$ 35,000	$ 47,500	$ 60,000
Large trade group	$100,000	$300,000	$500,000
Corporate lobbyist	$ 36,000	$ 60,000	$120,000
Manufacturing			
Foreman	$ 32,240	$ 40,300	$ 48,360
Purchasing agent	$ 42,240	$ 52,800	$ 63,360
Warehouse manager	$ 41,231	$ 53,600	$ 65,969
Director of engineering	$ 57,231	$ 74,400	$ 91,569
Manager of materials	$ 57,308	$ 74,500	$ 91,692
Plant manager	$ 77,462	$100,700	$123,938
VP for manufacturing	$106,231	$138,100	$169,969
Marketing			
Marketing assistant	$ 18,900	$ 24,000	$ 30,000
Market research manager	$ 45,700	$ 57,000	$103,000
Brand manager	$ 45,000	$ 61,000	$109,125
Direct-marketing manager	$ 40,000	$ 66,000	$110,000
VP for marketing	$109,250	$146,050	$212,750
Media			
Newspaper reporter	$ 21,856	$ 24,127	$ 37,113
Senior editor	$ 28,800	$ 41,900	$ 76,000
Managing editor	$ 28,400	$ 44,000	$210,000
Executive editor	$ 43,100	$ 52,800	$443,000
Book editor	$ 21,000	$ 44,090	$ 72,990
TV news reporter	$ 16,560	$ 30,400	$ 92,688
TV news anchor	$ 25,453	$ 65,824	$248,183
Movie producer	$400,000	$ 1,000,000	$5,000,000
Movie director	$ 50,000	$300,000	$500,000
Middle management	$ 50,035	$ 69,675	$151,165

Profession	Initial pay	Typical	Top Pay
Public relations			
Publicity agent	$ 19,210	$ 49,877	$ 66,467
In-house publicist	$ 23,400	$ 55,480	$ 62,613
Sales			
Sales trainee	$ 19,800	$ 30,700	$ 35,400
Sales representative	$ 38,900	$ 48,400	$ 59,900
Sales manager	$ 55,800	$ 65,300	$ 80,300
District sales manager	$ 64,900	$ 74,800	$ 88,100
Regional sales manager	$ 81,400	$ 95,000	$116,400
VP for sales	$136,100	$178,200	$226,900
Secretary	$ 12,480	$ 28,189	$ 50,000
Receptionist	$ 13,000	$ 22,387	$ 28,000
Executive secretary	$ 14,000	$ 37,485	$ 70,000
Investment banking			
Generalist	$ 95,000	$440,000	$ 1,250,000
M&A specialist	$ 95,000	$590,000	$ 1,750,000
Trader			
General instruments	$ 60,000	$290,000	$1,000,000
Foreign exchange or			
derivatives specialist	$ 60,000	$360,000	$2,000,000
Risk manager	$450,000	$725,000	$1,000,000
Retail stockbroker	$ 50,000	$150,000	$620,000
Institutional stockbroker	$ 88,000	$345,000	$1,000,000

(Source for above salary chart: *Fortune*, 6/26/95)

Hot Employment Trends for the Year 2000

Salary may be one of the major factors weighing on your mind when considering leaving the law. But you also need to have a bit more foresight than that. In addition to learning about salaries in other professions, you'll want to do some research into what the growth areas are for the present and the next five-to-ten years. It will make accomplishing your career transition much easier if the field you go into needs to hire people!

For each field listed below, the "hot track" (the specialty area within a field where growth is predicted) is cited, along with entry-, mid-, and top-level salary information.

ACCOUNTING

International Accountant

Entry Level:	$28,000–$32,250
Mid-level:	$43,000–$62,500
Top:	$55,000–$84,500

ARCHITECTURE

Design/Building Specialist

Entry Level:	$30,300
Mid-level:	$44,900
Top:	$61,500+

CONSULTING

Human Resources Professional

Entry Level:	$40,200
Mid-level:	$43,700
Top:	$62,000

Executive-Search Consultant

Entry Level:	$50,000–$60,000
Mid-level:	$150,000–$200,000
Top:	$300,000–$500,000

CONSTRUCTION

Construction Manager

Entry Level:	$29,000–$35,000
Mid-level:	$41,000–$52,000
Top:	$70,000+

EDUCATION

Special-Education Teacher (Public School)

All Levels:	$25,000–$50,000

Specialist in English as a Second Language

Entry Level:	$21,900
Midlevel:	$25,200
Top:	$40,500

Training Manager

Entry Level:	$30,000
Midlevel:	$45,000–$60,000
Top:	$65,000–$80,000

ENGINEERING

Chemical Engineer

Entry Level:	$23,000–$37,000
Midlevel:	$47,000–$62,000
Top:	$80,000+

Software Engineer

Entry Level:	$30,000
Midlevel:	$45,000
Top:	$60,000

ENTERTAINMENT

Computer Animator

Entry Level:	$27,000–$40,000
Midlevel:	$40,000–$80,000
Top:	$80,000+

ENVIRONMENT

Computer Mapper

Entry Level:	$26,000–$35,000
Midlevel:	$45,000–$50,000
Top:	$75,000+

Environmental Economist

Entry Level:	$30,000
Midlevel:	$50,000
Top:	$100,000+

INVESTMENT

Investment Manager

Entry Level	$40,000–$55,000
Midlevel:	$110,000–$160,000
Top:	$175,000–$325,000

HEALTH CARE

Dentist

Entry Level:	$50,000–$70,000
Midlevel:	$80,000–$100,000
Top:	$100,000–$207,000

Geriatric-Rehabilitation Therapist

Entry Level:	$35,000–$40,000
Midlevel:	$60,000
Top:	$85,000+

Information Specialist

Entry Level:	$27,500
Midlevel:	$47,500
Top:	$82,500

Internist in Infectious Diseases
Entry Level:	$117,048
Midlevel:	$145,300
Top:	$214,637

Obstetrician-Gynecologist
Entry Level:	$125,000
Midlevel:	$172,000
Top:	$200,000+

Psychopharmacologist
Entry Level:	$26,000–$52,000
Midlevel:	$65,000
Top:	$80,000

Registered Medical-Records Administrator
Entry Level:	$28,000
Midlevel:	$34,000
Top:	$90,000

Veterinarian
Entry Level:	$31,000
Midlevel:	$34,000
Top:	$150,000+

HOSPITALITY

Food Service Manager
Entry Level:	$30,000
Midlevel:	$37,000
Top:	$48,000

HUMAN SERVICES

Residential Counselor

Entry Level:	$15,000-$23,000
Midlevel:	$18,000-$27,000
Top:	$25,000-$35,000

INFORMATION

Business-Software Designer

Entry Level:	$42,000
Midlevel:	$57,000
Top:	$100,000

Online Content Developer

Entry Level:	$25,000-$35,000
Midlevel:	$50,000
Top:	$100,000

Web Master

Entry Level:	$50,000
Midlevel:	$75,000
Senior:	$100,000+

LAW

Biotech-Patent Lawyer

Entry Level:	$32,000-$60,000
Midlevel:	$125,000-$160,000
Top:	$160,000-$210,000+

Employment Lawyer

Entry Level:	$43,262
Midlevel:	$63,001-$77,131
Top:	$173,774-$191,300

Health Lawyer

Entry Level:	$40,000–$80,000
Midlevel:	$80,000–$120,000
Top:	$160,000–$240,000

MEDIA

Online Content Developer

Entry Level:	$25,000–$35,000
Midlevel:	$50,000
Top:	$80,000

MEDICINE

Wireless Salesperson

Entry Level:	$41,000
Midlevel:	$50,000–$60,000
Top:	$70,000

SCIENCE RESEARCH

Genetic Counselor

Entry Level:	$30,000
Midlevel:	$50,000
Top:	$85,000

Genetic Researcher

Entry Level:	$47,000
Midlevel:	$60,000
Top:	$80,000

SOCIAL WORK

Geriatric Case Manager

Entry Level:	$30,000
Midlevel:	$36,000
Top:	$45,000

SPORTS MANAGEMENT

Corporate Sales Representative

Entry-level: $18,000

Midlevel: $60,000

Top: $80,000+

TELECOMMUNICATIONS

Computer Security Expert

Entry Level: $30,000–$40,000

Midlevel: $65,000–$78,000

Top: $90,000+

Telecommunications Marketer

Entry Level: $30,000–$50,000

Midlevel: $45,000–$80,000

Top: $100,000+

(Sources: *Working Woman*, July/August, 1996; *U.S. News & World Report*, 1995)

NEGOTIATING SALARY TRANSITIONS

Of the many questions you have about leaving the practice of law, one of the most obvious is probably this: "Will I have to start at the bottom and take an entry level-salary?"

The answer to that question depends on 1) your previous experience, and 2) your ability to negotiate on your own behalf.

Unlike "lock-step" law firm salary structures, your salary in another profession may greatly depend on how well you sell yourself. While your new employer may not be getting a seasoned professional, they are not getting a recent college graduate either. They will be hiring a lawyer.

But since you are at the point of salary negotiation, clearly you have convinced them that it would be an asset to their organization to have someone with a law degree. If nothing else, they will presume that you are intelligent and hardworking enough to graduate from law school and pass the bar exam!

You do have some built-in credibility as a lawyer. You can capitalize on this, and on your transferable skills (see chapter 4) in salary negotiations. One of the most effective bits of career advice I have heard is that you should pretend that you are your own agent when conducting salary negotiations (in your own head, it's not necessary to do so out loud!). Try it right now—it's much easier to argue on your own behalf when you step "outside" of yourself and look objectively at your qualifications.

If you are asked how much you want to make, the first thing you should do is turn the question around and ask, "What is the salary range for this position?" If you are forced to name a number, give a range of at least five to ten thousand dollars (or more, depending on the typical salary in that field). Then you give yourself some margin of error and cut down your risk of getting underpaid/pricing yourself out of the market.

The salary charts in this chapter (pp. 12–16 and pp. 16–18) should give you an idea of what you might expect to earn in another profession. Industry associations are also always a good source of salary information. Most important, be prepared— go into salary negotiations with as much information as you can about the employer. What do they pay entry-level candidates? How about lateral movers? Consult their annual report, their internet site (if they have one), and anyone you know, including alums and the career planning department of your alma mater, to see if they have any information.

You also need to have a "bottom line." If you have done the monthly budget chart in this chapter, you'll know roughly how much money you need to live on. You also know if you can afford a temporary drop in salary. Having as much information about the employer's salary structure and your own financial picture should make you more confident during the negotiations.

You also need to be very aware that there other things for which you can negotiate besides money. Many employers are unwilling, or often unable, to move a lot in terms of your starting salary level. Other things, however, are often negotiable. For instance, you can negotiate for a better *title* in lieu of money. Some of the other most important negotiable items are *time and benefits*. You may be able to negotiate for more time off, or a different schedule, which may include: flex-time, time off without pay, a sabbatical, different hours. You may be able to negotiate for additional benefits such as training, reimbursement for continuing education, association memberships, company credit cards, business travel, or meal/car service reimbursement. The third thing you may be able to negotiate is more money later—*after you have proved yourself.* If you are not happy with your starting salary, see if there is potential for an early salary review—in six months, instead of one year.

Obviously, you have to be diplomatic when conducting salary negotiations. The time when you have the most power and persuasive ability is in between the time of offer and acceptance (you remember that from Contracts class, don't you?). That is when they have decided that they really want you and don't want to do another candidate search. But you have to be nice about it. A good idea and a diplomatic gesture is to be willing to give up something from your list gracefully—have a throw-away item that you do not consider crucial. Always continue to *strongly* express your enthusiasm for the new job throughout salary discussions. Do not forget to thank the employer for the opportunity when negotiations have concluded.

Finally, always put yourself in a position where you will know what to do if your salary requirements are not met. Are you willing to walk away without the job? Or do you want it so much that you will take it even if the salary is disappointing? Do you have any other interviews or offers pending? Psychologically, it is easier to negotiate on your own behalf when you don't feel desperate. How do you accomplish that? By sending out your resume and continuing to have networking meetings even when you are negotiating—until the "deal" is finalized, or you have accepted their offer.

Transitional Strategies

SELF ASSESSMENT: WHAT DO YOU WANT TO BE IF YOU'RE NOT A PRACTICING ATTORNEY?

The first step in starting a career transition is to look within yourself. Many people make the mistake of looking only to the job market. They look through the classified ads or call headhunters. They look for what "they can get." They don't spend any time thinking about what they really want—or how to figure out a way to position themselves so they can get it.

This is especially true in the realm of alternative legal careers. Attorneys come to me for counseling time and again, asking, "What else can I do?" as if there were an actual list of open jobs for lawyers who are unhappy practicing law. I don't blame them for asking—I would, too. But *any* type of job search, especially a transition out of law practices requires some self-assessment first. Without it, unfortunately, you may be heading right from the proverbial frying pan into the fire.

Self-assessment exercises can help you determine your strengths and interests, and can actually be a lot of fun and not very time consuming. For lawyers, it's especially helpful to let the creative juices flow, as you have probably been working so hard lately that you haven't had much time to reflect.

EXERCISE #1: LAWYER REALITY CHECK

This exercise is designed to help you determine how the "reality" of practicing law gels with your expectations for yourself prior to becoming a lawyer.

1. When did you decide to become a lawyer?

   When I was living in northern VA.

2. Why did you go to law school?

   I wanted to make a difference, I thought it would give me confidence, Joey was going, I was interested in politics.

3. How did you like law school?

   I really liked law school — the lectures opened up an entire new world for. However, I didn't like reading, drafting, researching or speaking!

4. How do you like practicing law?

   I hated it 99% of the time

   (a) What do you like about it?

   I liked it when I thought I was making a difference, I liked it when people appreciated my work, it gave me confidence.

(b) What do you dislike about it?

<u>It was tedious, unpredictable, I didn't fee</u>
<u>appreciated, I had no confidence</u>

(c) What would you want to change?

<u>I want to feel like I know what I'm doing</u>
<u>(confidence) I want to feel passion.</u>

5. If you didn't practice law, what else would you want to do?

<u>finance, project work, event planning, public</u>
<u>policy, campaign work, world bank</u>

6. If you had to stay in law, what changes in your environment, substantive area of practice, geographic location, employer, would you like to make? (*Circle all that apply.*)

Public

Private

Small

Large

Solo practice

Different substantive practice area

Different city or state

Work with different types of people

Completing Exercise #1 should: (a) help you figure out what went wrong and why; and (b) help you determine if you can fix it within law practice or by leaving for a new career. The responses could range from your realization that you *never* really wanted to be a lawyer, to a clash between your expectations of law practice and your current reality (which you may or may not be able to change to your satisfaction).

It is important to look back at your responses several times over a period of a week or longer to see if your feelings remain the same. You might want to add to or modify your answers. It would be helpful to discuss what you wrote with a friend, colleague, or a career counselor.

EXERCISE #2: BRAINSTORMING

Now that you have a greater understanding of your career in law, the brainstorming in Exercise #2, will give you an opportunity to think about and write down what you might like to do if you no longer practiced law. Really let yourself go. (I promise that it's not a binding document!)

_____

_____

_____

_____

EXERCISE # 3: CREATIVE VISUALIZATION

This exercise is designed to focus the brainstorming you did in Exercise #2 and give you a more concrete idea of your interests and values, while forcing you to think a little bit more about your choices.

1. A mysterious, anonymous donor has deposited $2 million in your bank account. Your money worries are over. What would you do if:

    (a) You quit your job and decided not to work for a year, but instead to enjoy a life of leisure?

    _____

    _____

    _____

    (b) You quit your job and are free from money worries, but you still want to work?

    _____

    _____

    _____

(c) There has been a binding stipulation made by the anonymous donor that the money must be donated to the cause(s) of your choice?

_____

_____

2. The same mysterious donor has given you $2 million, with the stipulation that you use it to start up a business. It can be any kind of business, including non-profit. You can use the money to rent office space, hire employees, buy equipment, or for any other purpose.

(a) What kind of business would you start?

_____

_____

_____

(b) Where would it be located?

_____

_____

_____

(c) What would your office look like (your personal office space)?

_____

_____

_____

(d) How many employees would you hire? What would be their function?

_____

_____

_____

3. The same wonderful donor has earmarked $50,000 of the money to be used to further your education. You can use it for anything from taking pottery classes at the local YMCA, to earning a doctorate from Harvard. What would you do with the money?

_____

_____

_____

4. Something terrible has happened. You have quit your job in reliance on the donor's money. Somehow it has all mysteriously disappeared. No one is able to help you out. Unemployment is unavailable. You must find something immediately.

   (a) What steps would you take to support yourself? What other skills do you have to rely on?

   _____

   _____

   _____

   (b) After working out an estimated annual budget, what is the bare minimum that you could live on? Be specific.

   _____

   _____

   _____

   (c) How much would it take for you to live comfortably?

   _____

   _____

   _____

5. Ten years from now, you have recovered your losses, and are being honored at a large black-tie dinner, to be televised worldwide.

   (a) What are you being honored for? (It can be an artistic, academic, political, sports-related, or any other type of award.).

   _____

   _____

   _____

   (b) Who is the first person you call? (You can only call one person.)

   _____

   _____

   _____

6. After receiving your award, your chauffeur drives you to the airport for the long flight home. Your flight is delayed so you go to the newsstand.

   (a) You purchase three newspapers/magazines. What are they?

   _____

   _____

   _____

   (b) Which articles do you turn to first? (Try to think about subject matter.)

   _____

   _____

   _____

EXERCISE # 4: SUNDAY PAPER "HELP WANTED" SURVEY

This exercise is designed to take all of the brainstorming and analyzing you have done above and apply it to the "real world" of jobs.

Go to your city's major Sunday paper's classified ads section. Grab your scissors, some tape, and some blank index cards. Read the entire section, from A to Z, cutting out anything that interests you. Tape each ad that you cut out to an index card. Highlight in red ink any information about job titles, responsibilities, qualifications needed, etc. Place the index cards in the order in which the positions interest you. Look it over every few days to see if you want to change the order of the cards. This should provide a wealth of ideas and possibilities for your future career. Keep the cards as a source of specific information for later when you might be looking for a job in any of these fields.

Once you have completed self assessment, you are ready to proceed to the next stage: research.

RESEARCHING A NEW CAREER: WHAT'S OUT THERE?

The first and most common question would-be career changers ask is, "What other job can I get with a law degree?" Although there are some common career paths, unfortunately, there is no list of other careers for which lawyers may get hired. There are, however, almost limitless resources for you to research other fields. Lawyers have been able to move into nearly every field that exists.

A good way to begin is to take a giant step back from the law, and read a good general resource book that surveys other fields in detail. A comprehensive book like *The Job Hunter's Sourcebook*, by Gale Research Inc., is an excellent place to start. This book outlines white-collar professions such as advertising, human resources, etc. Unless you know *exactly* what you want to do, this is a better way to start than to think about which other employers might want to hire lawyers. Just as a first-year law student might read a guide to law specialties to determine what exactly a labor lawyer does, you need to know the day-to-day details of what a creative director at an ad agency does before you can decide if it's for you, and how you might be able to position yourself to move into the field.

For each field described, the *Job Hunter's Sourcebook* has a comprehensive list of sources for help-wanted ads, placement and job referral services, employer directories, networking lists, and handbooks and other leads.

A great place to find general resources on specific careers, once you have done a general overview, is to start your research not in your law school, but in your *undergraduate career services* center, or one at a university in your region. Most schools have "reciprocity" with other colleges and universities, so that your career services center can get you permission to use a school in another part of the country. Most people do not realize that they can utilize their alma mater for information years after graduation.

Start by calling the Career Development or Career Services department of your school. (After you find career(s) in other fields that interest you, and research them thoroughly, your law school career counselor can additionally help you re-tool your resume and interviewing skills). After you visit your undergraduate school for resources, you should also stop by other graduate school career centers, (i.e., business school). They have good resources as well, and will usually let you in for a day or two if you are nice to them.

Below, you'll find a useful list of resources that should help you in your research on non-legal careers.

Advertising

Mogel, Leonard. *Making It in Advertising: An Insider's Guide to Career Opportunities*. New York: Collier Books, Macmillan Publishing Co., 1993.

Pattis, S. William. *Opportunities in Advertising Careers*. Lincolnwood, Illinois: VGM Career Horizons, 1985.

Arts

Eberts, Marjorie and Margaret Gisler. *Careers for Culture Lovers and Other Artsy Types*. Lincolnwood, Illinois: VGM Career Horizons, 1992.

Hanbenstock, Susan H. and David Joselit. *Career Opportunities in Art: A Comprehensive Guide to the Exciting Career Opportunities Open to You in Art*. New York: Facts on File Publications, 1988.

Langley, Stephen and James Abruzzo. *Jobs in Arts and Media Management: What They Are and How to Get One*. New York: American Council for the Arts Books, 1990.

Business

Axelrod, Alan S. and Paul D. Horvath, eds. *Harvard Business School Guide: Finance*. Cambridge, Massachusetts: Harvard Business School Press, 1994.

Career Choices for Students of Business. New York: Walker and Co., 1985.

Fischgrund, Tom, ed. *The Insider's Guide to the Top 20 Careers in Business and Management*. New York: McGraw Hill, Inc., 1994.

Nelson's Directory of Investment Research. Port Chester, New York: Nelson Publications, 1995.

Norback, Craig T., ed. *Handbook of Business and Management Careers*. Lincolnwood, Illinois: VGM Career Horizons, 1989.

Peterson's Job Opportunities in Business. Princeton, New Jersey: Peterson's, 1994.

Plunkett, Jack W. *Plunkett's Health Care Industry Almanac*. Galveston, Texas: Plunkett Research, Ltd., 1995.

Plunkett, Jack W. *Plunkett's InfoTech Industry Almanac*. Galveston, Texas: Plunkett Research, Ltd., 1996.

Ring, Trudy. *Careers in Finance*. Lincolnwood, Illinois: VGM Career Horizons, 1995.

Rosenthal, David W. and Michael Powell. *Careers in Marketing*. Engelwood Cliffs, New Jersey: Prentice Hall, Inc., 1984.

Selden, Ina Lee. *Going into Business for Yourself; New Beginnings After 50*. Glenview, Illinois: Scott, Foresman and Co., 1989.

Notes Payoff

For each field that you research, be sure to take notes on the following. You will need this information for interviewing, networking, resumes, and cover letters.
- Job description
- Job titles in field
- Major responsibilities
- Industry "buzz words"
- Salaries and industry forecast

Starr, Lila B. *Careers in Marketing*. Lincolnwood, Illinois: VGM Career Horizons, 1991.

Education

Edelfelt, Roy A. *Careers in Education*. Lincolnwood, Illinois: VGM Career Horizons, 1990.

Morgan, Bradley J. And Joseph M. Palmisano, eds. *Education Career Directory*. Detroit: Gale Research Inc., 1993.

Government

Career Choices for Students of Political Science and Government. New York: Walker and Co., 1985.

Close, Arthur C. and John P. Gregg, eds. *Washington Representative*. 11th edition. Washington, D.C.: Columbia Books, Inc., 1987.

Krannich, Ronald L. and Caryl Rae Krannich. *The Complete Guide to Public Employment*. Woodbridge, Virginia: Impact Publications, 1986.

Morgan, Bradley J. and Joseph M. Palmisano, eds. *Public Administration Career Directory*. Detroit: Visible Ink, 1994.

The United States Government Manual. Washington, D.C.: Office of the Federal Register, 1988.

International

Halloran, Edward J. *Careers in International Business*. Lincolnwood, Illinois: VGM Career Horizons, 1995.

Harlow, Victoria and Edward W. Knappman, eds. *American Jobs Abroad*. Detroit: Visible Ink, 1994.

Kocher, Eric. *International Jobs: Where They Are, How to Get Them*. Reading, Massachusetts: Addison-Wesley Publishing Co., 1993.

Krannich, Ronald L. and Caryl Rae Krannich. *Almanac of International Jobs and Careers; A Guide to Over 1001 Employers*. 2nd edition. Manassas Park, Virginia: Impact Publications, 1994.

Krannich, Ronald L. and Caryl R. Krannich. *The Complete Guide to International Jobs and Careers*. Manassas Park, Virginia: Impact Publications, 1992.

Looking for Employment in Foreign Countries. 9th edition. New York: World Trade Academy Press, 1992.

Sheehan, Gerard F., ed. *Careers in International Affairs*. Washington, D.C.: School of Foreign Service, Georgetown University, 1982.

Journalism

Guiley, Rosemary Ellen. *Career Opportunities for Writers*. New York: Facts on File Publications, 1991.

Journalist's Road to Success. Princeton, New Jersey: Dow Jones Newspaper Fund, 1994.

Morgan, Bradley J., ed. *Magazines Career Directory*. Detroit: Gale Research, Inc., 1993.

Tebbel, John. *Opportunities in Journalism*. Lincolnwood, Illinois: VGM Career Horizons, 1982.

Media

Blanksteen, Jane, and Avi Odeni. *TV Careers Behind the Screen*. New York: John Wiley and Sons, Inc., 1987.

Bone, Jane. *Opportunities in Cable Television*. Lincolnwood, Illinois: VGM Career Horizons, 1984.

Careers in Multimedia. Emeryville, California: Ziff-Davis Press, 1995.

Getting Started in Film: The Official American Film Institute Guide to Exciting Film Careers. New York: Prentice Hall, 1992.

Morgan, Bradley J., ed. *Radio and Television Career Directory*. Detroit: Gale Research, Inc., 1993.

Noble, John. *The Harvard Guide to Careers in Mass Media*. Cambridge, Massachusetts: President and Fellows of Harvard College, 1989.

U.S. Directory of Entertainment Employers. Van Nuys, California: Conumental Communications, 1996.

Publishing

Carter, Robert. *Opportunities in Book Publishing Careers*. Lincolnwood, Illinois: VGM Career Horizons, 1987.

Scherman, William H. *How to Get the Right Job in Publishing*. Chicago: Contemporary Books, Inc., 1983.

REAL-LIFE ALTERNATIVE CAREERS

The following is a list of agencies and positions that Class of 1995 law school graduates who reported selecting non-traditional legal and non-legal positions following graduation opted for. This list is based on a survey of recent law graduates conducted each year by the National Association for Law Placement.

1996 Olympics Committee
AARP
Account Representative
Actuarial Consulting
Administrative Assistant, Jury Commission
Adoption Agency
Adult Education Professor
Advertising
Aerospace Consultant
AIDS Law Center
Airline Management
Airline Mechanic
Alliance for Justice
Archdiocese of Detroit
Architect
Arizona Boys Town
Arms Control Association
Art Investment
Art Gallery
Asian Law Caucus
Assessor
Assistant to Township Manager
Assistant Controller at Law Firm
Assistant Chief- NH Liquor Enforcement

Assistant Director- Child Welfare Service
Associate Dean of Medical School
Association of Community Organizations
Athletic Club
Auditor
Bagel Industry
Bail Bondsman
Bailiff
Bar Association
Bartender
Bed and Breakfast Owner
Biochemist
Board of Healing Arts
Board of Tax Appeals
Board of Education
Bookstore
Botanical Garden
Boy Scouts of America
Business Owner/ Entrepreneur
Capitol Hill
Career Services
Carpentry
Caseworker
Catholic Charities

CEO of Hospital
Chapter 13 Trustee
Chef in Italian Restaurant
Chicago Housing Authority
Child Support Enforcement
Chiropractor
Church Director
City Legal Department
City Planner
Claims Supervisor
Clerk for Administrative
 Judge
Clinical Fellow - Medical
Coaching Mock Trials
Collection Agency
Collections Manager Trainee
College Financial Aid Office
College Librarian
College Admissions Office
Communications
Community Organization
Compliance Officer
Computer Consultant
Computer Software Training
Computer Systems Manager
Congressional Intern
Construction Worker
Coordinator—Domestic
 Violence Program
Copy Editor
Corrections Department
Council for Independent
 Living
Counselor for Troubled Teens
County Election Office
Court TV

Court Administration
CPA
Credit Card Recovery
Ship Crewperson
Criminal Appeals
Data Entry
Day Care
Dean of Planning
Defense Logistics Agency
Dental Legal Consultant
Dentist
Department of Social
 Services
Department of the Interior
Department of Public Health
 and Safety
Department of Energy
Design/Graphic Company
Detective-Sergeant—Portland
 Police
Development Director
Director of International
 Marketing
Director/Legal Counselor,
 State Commission
Director of Business
 Development
Director of State Prison
Disability Benefits Specialist
Docket Attorney at IRS
Drug Counseling Center
Magazine Editor
Educational Specialist, Train-
 ing Consultant
Election Board
Electronics Industry

Employment Specialist
Energy Conversion
  Development
Engineering Consultant
Environmental Consulting
EPA
Epidemiologist
Evidence Expert
Family Business
Family Court Counselor
FBI
Federal Elections
  Commission
Federal Reserve Bank
Federal Credit Union
Field Coordinator,
  Presidential Candidate
Financial Planner
Fireman
First Grade Teacher
Flight Attendant
Food Service
Football Team
Forest Service
Freelance TV Work
FTC
Fundraiser
Gambling Commission
Gas Research Institute
General Manager—Internet
  Marketing Firm
Governor's Office
Head Librarian—Fairfax Co.
  Public Schools
Health Policy Analyst

Health Care Finance
  Administration
High School Teacher
Home Care
Hospital Administration
Hospital Staff
Hotel Industry Consultant
House Committee on
  Commerce
Human Resources Manager
Image Consultant
Indian Tribe Attorney
Institute for International
  Affairs
Insurance Broker
Intake Officer for Mediation
  Program
Interior Designer
International Trading
  Company
Interpreter for Superior
  Court
Investigator
Investment Banker
Iowa Supreme Court
  Research
IRS
L.A. Times Circulation
  Manager
Lab Technician
Labor Counsel for East
  Bridgewater
Labor Relations
  Representative
Labor Union
Laboratory Specialist

Land Use Planner
Landscaping
Legal Document Support
  Service
Law Faculty Research
Legal Publishing
Legal Medicine—Air Force
Legislative Research
  Committee
Legislative Aide
Legislative Fiscal Bureau
Library of Congress
Litigation Support
Loan Originator
Lobbying
Lottery Board
Machine Operator
Major League Baseball
Management Intern
Management Consulting
Market Research
Maryland Homeless Program
Massachusetts Water
  Resource Authority
Math Teacher
Mayor's Office
Media Investment Company
Mental Health Counselor
Minnesota Pollution Control
Mitigation Team, Airport
  Expansion
Modeling
Mortgage Loan Officer
Motel Manager
Movie Industry Writer/
  Producer

Museum Teacher
Musician
National Center for State
  Courts
National Association of
  Securities Dealers
National Park Service
National Cancer Institute
Nature Conservancy
Naval Surface Warfare
Naval Air Warfare
Network Development
  Manager
Office Manager
Oil and Gas Title Work
Oil and Gas Business
Own/Operate Restaurant
  Chain
Paralegal Business
Paralegal
Parks Department Counsel
Pharmaceutical Company
Pharmacist
Police Officer
Police—Barrio Relations
Political Consultant
Port Authority
Portfolio Analyst
Prehearing Research
Printing Business
Produce Manager
Product Development
  Engineer
Production Company
Professional Photographers
Program Analyst

Protective Services for
  Adults
Public Guardian
Public Safety Director
Public Transit Authority
Rail Operations
Real Estate Development
Real Estate Appraisal
Real Estate Auction
Rebuild Consultant
Refugee Resettlement
Religious Instructor
Research Assistant
Retail Store Manager
Review Board, State
  Workforce Dept.
School of Mines
Search Firm
Securities and Exchange
  Commission
Security Guard
Self-Employment Inventor
Senior Product Developer
Service Specialist
Sheriff's Office
Shipping
Sierra Club
Snowboarding Business
Social Worker
Software Engineer
Special Education
Sports Management
Sports Marketing
State Assembly

Stock Trading
Substitute Teacher
Telemarketing
Texas State Board of Nurse
  Examiners
Therapist
Ticket Broker
Title Abstractor
Trainer of Thoroughbred
  Horses
Transit Authority
Travel Insurance
Trial Court Clerk
TV News Investigative Re-
  porter
University General Counsel's
  Office
University Intercollegiate
  Athletics Office
Urchin Diver
U.S. Postal Service
U.S. Department of Labor
U.S. Secret Service Special
  Agent
U.S. Department of Com-
  merce
Venture Capitalist
Visiting Nurse Association
Vista
Waiter
Wastewater Regulatory
YMCA Executive Director
Internet Resources

Of course, no section on research would be complete these days without information on the Internet. Even the most stodgy old law firms are developing their own websites and posting lateral job opportunities on the Internet. Legal recruiters, in particular, have also been utilizing the Internet to find candidates. A lot of quasi-legal positions that might interest you are posted online now by legal recruiters, government agencies, corporations, and *just* about any other employer. Check out some of the following listings for cyber-legal career information.

PRIMARY LEGAL AND QUASI-LEGAL POSITION WEBSITES

Law Journal Extra at http://www.ljx.com; Legal Employment Center link at http://www.lawjobs.com. Huge database with law, and law-related positions. You can browse by region or by state. Includes classified ads, law firm home pages, press releases, comprehensive listing of legal goods and services.

Counsel Connect Web at http://www.counsel.com; offered by American Lawyer Media; classified ads can be found at http://www.counsel.com/lawyers/class.html. Contains classified ads from the American Lawyer's publications nationwide and regionally (*Connecticut Law Tribune, New Jersey Law Journal, etc.*).

NON-LEGAL (GENERAL) JOB/CAREER WEBSITES

Careerpath: classified ads from nineteen major metropolitan newspapers, such as *The New York Times*, *Los Angeles Times*, and *Boston Globe*: found at http://www.careerpath.com.

Online Career Center: http://www.occ.com/occ/; Originally technical jobs for engineers, computer programmers—now has over 30 percent nontechnical positions.

America's Job Bank: http//www.ajb.dni.us/ Information on approximately 250,000 jobs. Search by occupation and state, or code or keyword search.

IN GENERAL

Use your web browser, go to http://www.yahoo.com/, click on business, then employment, then jobs—this will bring up a list of sites. Also, all of the commercial services such as America Online, Prodigy, and CompuServe have employment services online (CompuServe's ESpan is particularly well-known).

NETWORKING FOR ALTERNATIVE LEGAL CAREERS

Once you have completed self-assessment, and you have done your research, you are ready to set up networking meetings. The purpose of networking is to: a) gain advice and information; b) find out how you can better position yourself to get a job; and c) meet more people.

If you are a networking skeptic, you will be surprised how well this actually works. In fact, it is—statistically speaking—the best-known method for obtaining a real job. This is especially true when you are switching fields, since it may be harder to get a foot in the door with your resume alone. Although there are many ways to conduct a networking meeting, the easiest way to approach someone is to write them a short letter (do not enclose your resume) and then follow it up with a phone call. That way, they have some frame of reference for the reason you are calling. People will almost always be responsive as long as you are just asking for information and advice, not a job. Of course, they will remember you if a real job does come along—this happens more frequently than you may think.

Where to Find People to Network With:

- Alumni directories of your law school and undergraduate school
- Association lists (see list in this chapter)
- Newsletters/publications in the field
- Your friends, friends of friends, relatives, relatives of relatives, doctors, dentists, dry cleaners...ask everyone you know.

When you call, try to set up an in-person meeting if possible. Offer to buy them a cup of coffee or lunch (it never hurts to build up goodwill!). What to talk about? Ask them questions about themselves and how they got to where they are now. You'll be surprised to see your fifteen-minute meeting turn into a half-hour or more. During your appointment you may want to address:

A. Career:
   - their background
   - how their interest developed in this area
   - what they like best/least about the work
   - "career steps" (what former jobs they held, what they learned from each, how they progressed from one job to the next); if a former practicing lawyer, how the transition was made

B. Advantages and disadvantages of work
   - this field in different types of organizations (i.e., public sector, private sector, large, small)
   - this field in different parts of the country

C. What the organization is like and how it operates:
   - who they supervise, and report to
   - performance expectations
   - advancement opportunities
   - future growth potential/salary information (be diplomatic—ask for general information)

D. What organizations such as theirs are looking for in an employee.

E. What you could do to make yourself more attractive as a potential employee including:

- suggestions on upgrading your resume

- suggestions on interviewing techniques

- suggestions for additional educational and experiential qualifications you might pursue

- suggestions on where to go to find more information

- names of others in the field with whom you could speak

F. Do they know of any specific publications or job newsletters that contain job openings you should consider?

(Adapted in part from *Jobs for Lawyers,* Impact Publications, 1996)

NETWORKING SAMPLE LETTER OF INTRODUCTION

Name
Street Address
City, State Zip Code
Date

Contact Name
Title
Organization
Street Address
City, State Zip code

Dear _____ :

Amy Walsh suggested that I contact you about my interest in career opportunities in _____. I am a graduate of _____ Law School and _____ University. I have had several years of experience in _____.

(Your next paragraph should tell something about your background. Include your prior work experience, current situation, skills, interests, academic history, connection to the geographic region, etc.)

As I venture into the job market, I hope to benefit from the experience and knowledge of others in the field who might advise me on opportunities for someone with my qualifications. I would appreciate the opportunity to meet with you for 15 minutes for your guidance. I will call your office next week to see if we can schedule a meeting.

I look forward to discussing my plans with you.

Sincerely,

Jonathan Wright

Exploring Alternative Careers—An Abridged List of Related Associations

One of the best ways for you to network your way into a field other than law is to become a member of that field's association. This enables you to meet all of the key people in the field in a collegial, non-threatening environment. The following is a list of major associations in fields you may want to enter. It will also give you an idea of how many associations exist for every field.

FINANCIAL SERVICES

Accountants and Auditors

National Association of Accountants
10 Paragon Drive
P. O. Box 433
Montvale, NJ 27645

National Society of Public Accountants
1010 North Fairfax Street
Alexandra, VA 22314

Institute of Internal Auditors
249 Maitland Avenue
Altamonte Springs, FL 32701

American Society of Women Accountants
35 East Wacker Drive
Chicago, IL 60601

American Institute of Certified Public Accountants
1211 Ave. of the Americas
New York, NY 10036-8775

Banking Administrators and Managers

American Bankers
Association
Bank Personnel Division
1120 Connecticut Ave, NW
Washington, D.C. 20036

Bank Administration
Institute
60 Gould Center
Rolling Meadows, IL 60008

National Bankers Association
122 C Street, NW
Suite 240
Washington, D.C. 20001

Budget Analysts

U. S. Office of Personnel Management
1900 E Street, NW
Washington, D.C. 20415

Financial Planners and Managers

College for Financial Planning
9725 East Hampden Avenue
Denver, CO 80231

International Board of Standards & Practices
for Certified Financial Planners, Inc. (IBCFP)
5445 DTC Parkway, Suite P-1
Englewood, CO 80111

Investment Bankers

National Association of Securities Dealers
1735 K Street NW
Washington, D.C. 20006

Securities Industry Association
120 Broadway
New York, NY 10271

Loan Officers

American Bankers Association
Bank Personnel Division
1120 Connecticut Ave, NW
Washington, D.C. 20036

National Bankers Association
122 C Street, NW
Suite 240
Washington, D.C. 20001

Bank Administration
Institute
60 Gould Center
Rolling Meadows, IL 60008

Management Consultants

Association of Management Consultants
500 North Michigan Avenue
Chicago, IL 60611

Association of Management Consulting Firms, Inc.
230 Park Avenue
New York, NY 10169

Institute of Management Consultants
19 West 44th Street
New York, NY 10036

Securities Analysts

Institute of Chartered Financial Analysts
P. O. Box 3668
Charlottesville, VA 22903

Financial Analysts Federation
1633 Broadway, 16th Floor
New York, NY 10019

Securities Sales Representatives (Stockbrokers)
Securities Industry Association
120 Broadway
New York, NY 10271

INSURANCE AGENTS AND BROKERS

Life Insurance Agent or Broker
Insurance Institute of America
Providence and Sugartown Rds
Malvern, PA 19355

Casualty Insurance Agent or Broker
Insurance Information Institute
110 William Street
New York, NY 10038

Independent Insurance Agents of America
100 Church Street
New York, NY 10007

Professional Insurance Agents
400 North Washington Street
Alexandria, VA 22314

SALES AND MARKETING

Advertising Managers and Account Executives
American Association of Advertising Agencies
666 Third Avenue, 13th Floor
New York, NY 10017

American Advertising Federation
1400 K Street, NW
Suite 1000
Washington, D.C. 20005

Association of National Advertisers
155 East 44th Street
New York, NY 10017

American Marketing
Association
230 North Michigan Avenue
Chicago, IL 60606

Media Planners
American Advertising Federation
1400 K Street, NW
Suite 1000
Washington, D.C. 20005

American Association of Advertising Agencies
666 Third Avenue
13th Floor
New York, NY 10017

Public Relations Specialists
For job opportunities in public relations send $1 to:
Service Department
Public Relations News
127 East 80th Street
New York, NY 10021

Purchasing Agents and Managers
National Association of Purchasing Management, Inc.
2055 East Centennial Circle
P. O. Box 22160
Tempe, AZ 85282

Real Estate Agents and Brokers
American Society of Real Estate Counselors
430 North Michigan Avenue
Chicago, IL 60611

National Association of Realtors
430 North Michigan Avenue
Chicago, IL 60611

The National Association of Real Estate Brokers
5501 Eighth Street NW
Suite 202
Washington, D.C. 20011

National Institute of Realtors
Department of Education
155 East Superior Street
Chicago, IL 60611

Sales and Marketing Executives

American Marketing
Association
250 South Wacker Drive
Suite 200
Chicago, IL 60606-5819

Sales and Marketing Executives, International
446 Statler Office Tower
Cleveland, OH 44115

Wholesale and Retail Buyers

National Retail Merchants Association
100 West 31st Street
New York, NY 10001

ARCHITECTURE/ENGINEERING/COMPUTER SCIENCE

Chief Information Officers

Association for Systems Management
24587 Bagley Road
Cleveland, OH 44138

Civil Engineers

American Society of Civil Engineers
345 East 47th Street
New York, NY 10017

Computer Programmers

Data Processing Management Association
505 Busse Highway
Park Ridge, IL 60068

Association of Computer Programmers & Analysts
2108-C Gallows Road
Vienna, VA 22180

IEEE (Institute of Electrical and Electronics Engineers)
Computer Society
1730 Massachusetts Ave, NW
Washington, D.C. 20036

Microcomputer Software Association
1300 North 17th Street,
No. 300
Arlington, VA 22209

Association for Computing Machinery, Special Interest
Group on Programming Languages
11 West 42d Street
Third Floor
New York, NY 10036

Computer Security Specialists

Information Systems Security Association
P.O. Box 9457
Newport Beach, CA 92658

Computer Systems Analysts

Association for Systems Management
24587 Bagley Road
Cleveland, OH 44138

NATURAL SCIENCE AND MATHEMATICS

Mathematicians

American Mathematical Society
P. O. Box 6348
Providence, RI 02940
(send $2 for a booklet)

Mathematical Association of America
1529 18th Street, NW
Washington, D.C. 20036

Society for Industrial and Applied Mathematics
1400 Architects Building
117 South 17th Street
Philadelphia, PA 19103

Institute of Mathematical Statistics
3401 Investment Blvd, No. 7
Hayward, CA 94545

Science Technicians

American Chemical Society
Career Services
1155 16th Street, NW
Washington, D.C. 20036

Naomi Williams, President
National Conference of Chemical Technician
Affiliates of the American Chemical Society
Monsato Co., Q3D
800 North Lindbergh Blvd
St. Louis, MO 63167

American Institute of Biological Sciences
730 11th Street, NW
Washington, D.C. 20001

SOCIAL SCIENCES, THE LAW, AND LAW ENFORCEMENT

Alcohol and Drug Counselors

National Clearinghouse on Alcoholism & Drug Abuse
Information (NCADI)
P. O. Box 2345
Rockville, MD 20852

Alcohol and Drug Problems Association (ADPA)
444 North Capitol Street, NW
Suite 181
Washington, D.C. 20001

National Association of Alcoholism & Drug Abuse Counselors
(NAADAC)
3717 Columbia Pike
Suite 300
Arlington, VA 22204

National Association of Substance Abuse Trainers and
Educators (NAST) Southern University of New Orleans
Training Program for the Control of Substance Abuse
6400 Press Drive
New Orleans, LA 70126

Corporate Trainers

American Society for Training and Development
600 Maryland Avenue, SW
Suite 305
Washington, D.C. 20025

National Training Laboratory
P. O. Box 9155
Roslyn Station
Arlington, VA 22209

Economists
America Economic Association
1313 21st Avenue South
Nashville, TN 37212-2786

Joint Council on Economic Education
432 Park Avenue South
New York, NY 10016

National Association of Business Economics
28349 Chagrin Boulevard
Suite 203
Cleveland, OH 44122

Urban and Regional Planners
American Planning Association
1776 Massachusetts Avenue, NW
Washington, D.C. 20036

Association of Collegiate Schools of Planning
College of Design, Architecture, Art & Planning
University of Cincinnati
Cincinnati, OH 45221

National Planning Association
1616 P Street, NW
Suite 400
Washington, D.C. 20036

EDUCATION AND LIBRARY SCIENCE

Adult and Vocational Education Teachers
American Association for Adult and Continuing Education
1112 16th Street, NW
Suite 420
Washington, D.C. 20036

American Vocational Association
1410 King Street
Alexandria, VA 22314

Archivists and Curators

Society of American Archivists
600 South Federal Street
Suite 504
Chicago, IL 60605

American Association of Museums
1225 I Street, NW
Suite 200
Washington, D.C. 20005

Association of Art Museum Directors
41 East 65th Street
New York, NY 10021
American Association of Botanical Gardens and Arboreta
P. O. Box 206
Swarthmore, PA 19081

American Institute for Conservation of Historic and Artistic
Works
3545 Williamsburg La, NW
Washington, D.C. 20008

ADDITIONAL RESOURCES

Encyclopedia of Associations
Gale Research, Inc.
P.O. Box 33477
Detroit, MI 48323-5477
313-962-2242

Encyclopedia of Business Information
Gale Research, Inc.
P.O. Box 33477
Detroit, MI 48323-5477
313-962-2242

Directory of Trade Shows
312-579-9090

Association Meeting Directory
800-541-0663

Directory of On-Line Databases
Gale Research, Inc.
P.O. Box 33477
Detroit, MI 48323-5477

Directory of Consulting Organizations
313-962-2242

National Executive Search Corps
275 Park Avenue South
New York, NY 10010
212-529-6660

International Executive Service Corps
P.O. Box 1005
Stamford, CT 06904
203-967-6000

(*Adapted from *Jobs for Lawyers,* Impact Publications, 1996)

RESUME STRATEGIES FOR ALTERNATIVE LEGAL CAREERS

The magic of modern technology, combined with some crafty techniques, can enable you to transform your resume into one that can cross legal lines (so to speak). You must first realize that your resume is not a passive list of the jobs you have held— it is a *marketing tool.*

It should not look like the application you filled out to get admitted to the bar or an employment application. Yes, you do need to be 100 percent honest. And yes, you do need titles, dates, responsibilities, etc. But the rest is up to you. As you will see, how and where you place your experience on a resume, and how you describe it, can have a profound effect on the reader. You have the power to emphasize what you want, phrasing your descriptions in language that will "grab" the interviewer's attention.

BASIC RESUME RULES

- Whatever is on the top half of the page will receive more attention

- Whatever is on the left hand side of the page will usually be read first (the eye naturally reads from left to right) so don't waste your time putting less striking information, like the dates of employment in the left hand margin

- "Experience" sections can include volunteer experience as well as paid experience

- Education can go on the top half of the page or the bottom half, depending on what you want to emphasize

- There are no absolute rules—it's your resume and you have to be happy with it

QUASI-FUNCTIONAL RESUMES

A traditional chronological resume lists all of the positions you have held in reverse-chronological order. You probably have one of these on your computer. A functional resume simply groups your experience by skills sets, without giving much employment history information. A *quasi-functional* resume lists your relevant skills on top, and your employment history at the bottom. This can be an effective resume technique that you can use to present your credentials to an employer in a different industry.

"You have to present yourself in a way that makes sense to a prospective employer," says Linda E. Laufer, New York-based career expert. "The employer needs to think that it makes sense, logically, that you would be applying for this position." That's where a quasi-functional resume comes in. The first thing the employer reads relates to skills or experience that would be very desirable for the job that he or she has open.

So, if you are looking for a job as a legal editor, your first paragraph would be called "Editing" or "Writing" skills, and you would extrapolate everything you have written at various jobs, at schools you have attended, or personal side projects, and group it under that heading. (If you have no experience in your desired field, see chapter 5 for ideas on how to get some quickly.)

Or, let's say you are a litigator who wants to become a career counselor at a law school. What skills would the dean be on the lookout for? Well, counseling skills for sure. Marketing and public relations skills, interpersonal and public speaking skills would be important too. Finally, administrative skills are needed. Once you have found out the skills required by doing your research, you would group "Marketing/Public Relations" skills and "Administrative" skills in the top section of your resume, and describe what you have achieved in these areas.

Take out your most recent "legal" resume. To convert it to a "functional" format, fill out the following outline, grouping your skills. Highlight the ones that relate to new fields you are pursuing. Include everything that you have done through work or on a volunteer basis. Do not worry about the chronology. Use bullets and action verbs to make your point.

SKILLS FOR A FUNCTIONAL RESUME

Marketing: _____

Writing: _____

Public Speaking: _____

Counseling: _____

Business: _____

Then put it all together with your employment history listed on the second half of the page—listing names of employers, titles, and dates of employment only. Finally, have your education section at the bottom of the page, using the same basic format.

As resume strategies are always easier to understand when you see them, the resumes found on pp 140–150 (all based on real people) are designed to show you how to take your legal employment and turn it into a resume for a non-legal field.

Read them for format, style, and substance. Most of the sample resumes incorporate at least a partially functional format.

SAMPLE CHRONOLOGICAL LEGAL RESUME

Name
Address
Home Phone

Bar Status

Admitted in New Jersey and Connecticut
(or) Passed New York State; awaiting admission

Legal Experience

Employer Name   City, State
Your title   Dates
• Using bullets, describe your experience. Remember, use action verbs!

Employer Name   City, State
Your title   Dates
• Using bullets, describe your experience. Remember, use action verbs!

Additional Experience

Employer Name   City, State
Your title   Dates
• Using bullets, describe your experience. Remember, use action verbs!

Education

School Name
J.D., May 1991
Class Standing:
Honors:
Associate Editor, *Title of Journal* (Journal membership can
    also be listed under activities)
Dean's List
Activities: Name of Student Association, Public Service Project

School Name
B.A., cum laude, Month, year
Major: (List here)
Honors: (List here)
Activities: (List here)

PERSONAL

Interests include…

You can use the following Job Search Contact Form to keep a record of the resumes you have sent out and follow-up action you have taken with the potential employer (it's a good idea to make copies of the form or create your own version).

JOB SEARCH CONTACT FORM

Name of Employer: _____

Contact Person: _____

Date Contacted: _____

Action Taken: _____

_____

Outcome : _____

_____

_____

_____

_____

_____

INTERVIEWING FOR AN ALTERNATIVE LEGAL CAREER: OVERCOMING OBJECTIONS

When you interview for a non-legal position, you will not only be responding to the interview questions, you will be actively convincing them that they would benefit from hiring someone with a law degree. While for some positions, i.e., Legal Editing, it may be a required credential, for other positions you will be the first lawyer they have interviewed (and hopefully hired). You will be most likely overcoming their implicit, or explicit objections: Why don't you want to practice? Why would you want this job? How do I know you would be willing to take orders from me? Would you stay, or is this a temporary stop for you?

So, what do you do to allay their fears? You need to: a) *Address them*—you can bring up their unspoken objections yourself and give them assurances; and b) Always use positive, affirming language when answering their questions.

Example:

Interviewer: Why don't you want to practice law?

Interviewee: Wrong Response:

- Practicing law is not as glamorous as you think it is.

- The hours are really long!

- There have been a lot of layoffs recently.

- It can be boring at times.

Correct Response:

- I have enjoyed my five years of practice with X, Y, and Z. During my time there, I developed an interest in commercial real estate and have decided to pursue a full-time career as a real estate developer.

BUT...WHAT SKILLS DO YOU HAVE TO OFFER THEM?

Okay, so you can handle the initial objections. But what do you have to offer? In any part of the job search, from cover letters to interviews, your credo should be:"Ask not what the employer can do for you, but what *you* can do for the employer." So as a lawyer what can you bring to the table? Fortunately, lawyers have many skills that can be transferred to another profession. Below is a rundown of skills you probably take for granted, but that are very marketable—and very transferable to careers outside of the law:

- Problem Solving
- Research
- Writing
- Attention to Detail
- Drafting
- Reading the fine print
- Working hard
- Negotiation
- Persuasion
- Public Speaking
- Listening/Counseling
- Interviewing (both prospective clients and associates)
- Evaluating
- Managing/Supervising
- Juggling multiple projects/tasks
- Logic
- Working well under deadline pressure
- Strategic Thinking/Planning
- Client Development/Rainmaking

Depending on your area of practice, some or all of these will apply to you. It's a good idea to point these skills out to the interviewer, by way of examples from your past work (trial work, discovery, deals, etc.), and then relate them to the position for which you are interviewing.

USING INDUSTRY BUZZ WORDS IN INTERVIEWS

Finally, once you have overcome the interviewer's initial wariness and highlighted your transferable skills, you need to "talk the talk" of the new industry you are in. Not in it yet? Well, act as if you were already in the club, and use the language, or industry "buzz words" that your interviewer recognizes. As legal career expert, Linda E. Laufer says, "You have to get it ("the character, or the new career") in your bones...You have to be able to envision yourself in the position first before others can effectively view you in it."You will have learned industry buzz words from your previous research and networking meetings. You should also refer back to the index cards you completed in Self-Assessment Exercise # 4 from the classified ads for industry terms and phrases.

Example: What if you wanted to become an entertainment industry scriptwriter, like the lawyer who became the head writer for *L.A. Law* in the 1980s? Well, if you were out on the coast interviewing, you would not want to be talking depositions and briefs. You would want to be talking loglines, treatments, and "high concept."

Once you have mastered basic industry terminology in this, or any other field with confidence, your job interviews will start to flow more naturally. Having convinced the interviewer of your fluency and grasp of the industry, you will make a better candidate for any open position.

Making It Happen: Initial Steps Out

By this time, you have learned how to restructure your resume to apply for a non-legal position, how to network and interview, and how make yourself marketable to other, non-legal positions through research; but you may not be ready to leave the law cold turkey. Or, you may have an intuitive feeling that you *do* like law, but you really just need a change of pace. Or you may have decided that law is not the problem at all, but that you need to spend less time at it, so you have time for more of a life.

This chapter is about small steps that you can take away from practicing law, which will help push you out of it for good, or back into it, but perhaps with a modification to your lifestyle. They are all less risky than leaving law entirely, but big enough to make a difference in your life and have an impact on your ultimate decision.

A Few Words About Change

This book is all about change. The change from lawyer to non-practicing lawyer is a big one—frightening, emotional, and at the same time liberating. This chapter will help make the change—and the fear that goes with it—more manageable.

Before taking the giant leap from law, you can first take some "baby steps." These are all transitional steps, designed to build up your resume, experience, and your courage. Remember, change is hard, even if the end result is to make you happier.

A first step toward deciding to leave law practice may involve taking an extended vacation. You may be so burned out that you need to catch your breath first, before even attempting a career change. Maybe you just need a break, a change of pace, before committing yourself one way or the other. The two weekends you were away last year barely scratched the surface.

Whether it's a two-week summer vacation or a six-month sabbatical, it can: 1) provide a crucial sense of perspective; and 2) give you an opportunity to research a new career, or experience short-term what it would actually be like to be in that career. Sometimes when you are completely stuck, it can be a relief to try something on a small scale first, before making any final decisions. Chances are, time off will clarify your decision, either providing a break from a high-stress career, or proving that you need to leave once and for all.

Change Is a Process

"Once change has occurred, we find ourselves disoriented, grief stricken, confused ... even in the face of good changes. These feelings are part of a process called transition ... Transition takes a long time because there are many parts to it."

(From "Why Even Good Changes Can Make Us Feel Bad," by Ruth Luban, MA., from *Lawyers in Transition* newsletter, July-September 1992, published by Hindi Greenberg.)

How Can You Possibly Get Away?

As a lawyer, you are used to working some of the hardest, longest hours of any profession. How are you going to get away long enough to research or even experience a new career, much less get home one night in time for dinner. Well, to start with, legal employers generally do have generous vacation policies—typically three to four weeks.

Is there a way you can take as much time as possible in one chunk? If you've just completed a deal/settled a trial, or are in a practice area that has some downtime at distinct times of year (i.e., tax, trusts and estates), maybe you can do it. The problem seems to be that most lawyers are so involved in the daily grind, there's no time to plan your mini career-change vacation.

Fortunately, I have done the research for you. All you have to do is read this chapter, make a few phone calls, and convince yourself to do it. After all, if you don't, you'll never know what else might have been. As they say, on your deathbed you won't regret that you did not spend more time at the office—trite but true.

One caveat: It is imperative that you disconnect yourself as much as possible from the firm during your mini-sabbatical—literally. Little or no interaction via fax, cellular phone, voice mail, or e-mail is important, or it will not be as possible for you to focus on your own needs. Try to arrange for someone else to cover for you in the office. The hardest part of planning the whole vacation will be proving to your colleagues, and to yourself, that they can and will survive your short-term absence.

MINI-SABBATICALS/RETREATS AND CAREER-CHANGE VACATIONS

There are places where you can go to rethink your career, oftentimes for as little as a week. Half the price of a week at a spa, and a hundred times more useful than a week at Club Med, they are a great invention for people like lawyers, who don't get a lot of time off. They are run by trained career counselors, and are often held as mini-retreats in beautiful settings. If nothing else, it will give you a chance to clear your mind, and focus one hundred percent on yourself for a short time. Listed below are some of the best.

Centerpoint

Centerpoint Institute for Life and Career Renewal has two distinct advantages: It has lawyer-friendly programs and it is located in Seattle, a beautiful place to decide your future. John Hart, the White House official profiled in this book, attended a Centerpoint retreat shortly before making the decision to leave law for politics. They run programs in their office in Seattle and retreats held at mountain or waterfront lodges in the countryside outside of Seattle during the summer and fall months.

Centerpoint is run by Carol Vecchio, a career counselor for attorneys, and former career planning director at a major law school, and Rikk Hansen, a career development expert. Centerpoint offers seminars specifically for dissatisfied/burned-out lawyers at their main office in Seattle, and their costs are fairly reasonable. For more information on Centerpoint, write: CENTERPOINT, 1326 Fifth Avenue, 658 Skinner Building, Seattle, WA. 98101-2604. Phone number: (206)-622-8070.

Richard Bolles's Career Vacation/Retreats

Richard Bolles, the "daddy" of all career counseling, and the author of the best selling book *What Color is Your Parachute* offers a retreat once a year for job/career changers. Most recently, the retreat has been held at the Inn of the Seventh Mountain in Oregon. For more information, write: Registrar, Two Week Workshop, *What Color is Your Parachute*, P.O. Box 379l, Walnut Creek, CA 94597.

The Crystal Barkley Institute

Although it is not a vacation or a retreat, the Crystal Barkley Institute (main headquarters in New York City, locations throughout the country), offers intensive, one-week career change programs that are highly regarded. They are, however, pretty expensive. For more information, call (800) 333-9003, or in NY, call (212) 889-8500 or write: 152 Madison Ave., 23rd floor, NY 10016. Their intensive forty-hour seminars are offered several times a year in Atlanta, Los Angeles, and Chicago. In New York, they do not offer a five-day seminar, but they do offer the intensive forty-hour course on two sequential weekends. John Crystal, the Institute's founder, was Richard Bolles's original mentor. Follow-up consulting is mandatory. The course costs $1,430 and includes five hours of private counseling. If you register 30 days in advance, you'll receive a 10 percent discount, so it's a good idea to plan ahead. If you decide that the course isn't exactly what you need, there is also private counseling available for $150/hour.

LONGER VACATIONS/SABBATICALS

Sometimes, two weeks away is not enough. Ideally, your time away should be a month or more. Has a lawyer ever been able to do this? Believe it or not, yes. Unfortunately, it is more precedented at the partner level than at the associate level. If you are currently an associate, you may have to settle for a mini-retreat/vacation (described above), or a series of weekend seminars. If you are well-liked in the firm, however, you might be able to initiate a sabbatical program for associates.

HOW TO CONVINCE THE PARTNERS

It may be a tough sell at first, but here are some tips. Let us say that you are a fifth-year associate at a law firm. Convince the firm to form a sabbatical policy, starting with you. Then, remind the other associates and partners that if you can go, they can go too. If you are willing to take an unpaid sabbatical, you can argue that you will save the firm money (no lawyer can argue with that). If you are planning to do volunteer work/community service, you can convince the firm that it will be good for public relations. In this era of downsizing, law firms are increasingly willing to consider alternative work arrangements as a cost-cutting measure.

Sound too good to be true? If you are feeling like you could not possibly take leave, work could not survive without you, the firm would never let you, etc., here is some food for thought. This time off may be *necessary* to your mental and physical health. If you are seriously burned out, you risk doing your body harm. In addition, I *strongly recommend* that if you are at a loss as to whether or not to leave practice, you give time-off a try. It may be the only way for you to gain perspective, and then make a final, well-thought-out decision.

WHAT IF THEY WON'T LET YOU GO?

If you can't swing it, you have some tough choices ahead. How about quitting outright? It is obviously a big risk and may not be possible if you have student loans. But if you have a spouse who is employed and you don't have any major debt, don't rule it out completely. Many, many lawyers have struggled with these issues. Among those who have quit completely, Glen Gulino (profiled in chapter 6) is now an agent for William Morris. Even though Glen's story is a successful one, it took him a few years to get on track, and he even used some of his savings to tide him over. Others have temped or subcontracted projects to law firms. Another made a deal with her spouse to take a year off and has now started a career in advertising. It's not easy, but it isn't impossible, either (For more encouragement, see *Utne Reader*'s "Just Quit! The Fine Art of Breaking Free," October, 1996.)

FINANCING YOUR TIME AWAY

Whether for two weeks or six months, whether paid or unpaid, you have decided that you need to do this. Hopefully, you have been able to arrange it without alienating your employer and your family. You are nervous but excited. Fortunately, you are not the first person to decide to do this. What follows is a resource list of organizations people have used to get partial funding, and stories of real-life lawyers who have actually taken sabbaticals. Some are still lawyers, and others have left the profession.

Although some of the following organizations were started primarily to help college students find financial aid or nonprofits find funding, they also help individuals and are an often over-looked source of actually providing some income for your time away.

The National Scholarship Research Service, 2280 Airport Boulevard, Santa Rosa, CA. 95403. (707) 546-6781. President: Dan Cassidy. Provides custom database searches of fellowships, grants, and scholarships for a range of fees. Primarily oriented to funding college or graduate school but will help with individual fellowships.

The Foundation Center, (212) 620-4230 or (800) 424-9836 (for book orders only). Main offices in NY; centers in other major cities including Atlanta and Honolulu. The Foundation Center is a library where you can do the research yourself instead of paying a fee for having the research done. They have a good amount of information in the area of foundation grants to individuals.

The Center For Interim Programs, Cambridge, MA. (617) 547-0980. For a set fee of approximately $1,500, the center provides consultation, counseling, and program advice over a two-year period to college students, academics, and others interested in spending time away.

What to Do on Your Sabbatical

Here are some ideas to get you started, based on what other attorneys have done with their time off:

- Volunteer
- Travel
- Write
- Do an internship
- Have an outdoors adventure
- Study a language abroad
- Work on a political campaign
- Do community service or pro bono work
- Do something artistic
- Pursue whatever you really liked to do before you went to law school

For more information on taking a sabbatical, check out *Time Off From Work*, by Lisa Angowski Rogak, John Wiley & Sons, 1994, and *Six Months Off*, by Hope Delogozina, James Scott, and David Sharp, Henry Holt, 1996.

Annual Register of Grant Support. A Directory of Funding Sources, R.R. Bowker, Providence, NJ (908) 464-6800. A listing of almost 3,000 programs sponsored by different types of organizations. Cost: approximately $175.00

LAWYERS ON SABBATICAL: WHERE DO THEY GO?

THE PARTNERS AT DEBEVOISE & PLIMPTON

Debevoise, a large, prestigious firm based in New York, is one of the only firms that has a standardized sabbatical policy. It is only available to partners. However, among the partnership, it has been very well utilized since its inception in 1981. Partner sabbaticals often include travel and/or learning a foreign language in the country in which it is spoken. The sabbatical can be taken once during the partner's career, lasts from four to six months, and is paid up to four months. There is no requirement that the sabbatical be used in any particular way; however, there is an application requirement and a committee that oversees the process to insure the sabbaticals are staggered properly.

Presiding Partner Barry Bryan took his to spend time at his home on Fisher's Island. Lawyer/writer/partner Louis Begley, Jr. took his sabbatical to write his award-winning novel, *Wartime Lies*. Partner Barbara Robinson used her time to become an apprentice in a well-known English garden. Both the partners and the firm's clients have found a way to make the sabbatical policy workable. "We are happy with the program," said presiding partner Bryan. "The anticipated disruption gets absorbed quite well, and the clients are very supportive in general." A concerted effort on the part of the firm to do a lot of advance planning is a key to its success.

THE CENTER FOR INTERIM PROGRAMS

The Center for Interim Programs in Boston assists people in deciding where and how to go on sabbatical and is aware of programs in nearly every part of the world, ranging from tallship training in the Caribbean, to studying art history in Italy.

Interim (see more information in Financing Your Time Away, p. 76) has "assisted a steady stream of 'burned out lawyers'...who are casting about for opportunities," according to its founder, Cornelius Bull.

With the planning expertise of Bull, Maine attorney Peter Plumb took a year off in 1989 to travel with his family—six months sailing the South Pacific, followed by six months in Nepal. The trip was a success, and his career got right back on track in the years following his return. "Lawyers are the worst," said Plumb. "They are so fearful that their clients will desert them." In fact, the trip had a "negligible" effect on his clients and practice and Plumb, who now lives for part of the year on an island off the coast of Portland, has incorporated more pleasure into his life since the sabbatical. "I don't let myself get as stressed out as I used to," he said. Of the twelve lawyers in his firm, three of them have now taken sabbaticals.

MAJOR CORPORATIONS/LEGAL ORGANIZATIONS

Many law firms and other companies with in-house legal departments are jumping on the sabbatical bandwagon. Below you'll find a list of some major corporate players that are getting their employees to stay by letting them go:

Corporations
(Approximate size of legal department is indicated):

Apple Computers (36)

American Express (67)

I.B.M. (195)

Time Warner (148)

Nike (7)

McDonalds (74)

Lotus (10)

Federal Express (59)

Xerox (74)

Legal Organizations:

U.S. Department of Justice

Most Universities and Law Schools

Heller Ehrman White & McAuliffe

Bronson, Bronson & McKinnon

COUNSELING

Seeking some form of short-term counseling, either through individual or group career counseling or therapy, can be a good way to clarify your feelings and decide which direction suits you best.

CAREER COUNSELING

If you are truly stuck, career counseling can be very, very helpful in clarifying your career goals. Career counseling can be short–or long-term, ranging from one session to ongoing sessions over a period of several months. Career counselors use a combination of self-assessment inventories, coaching, information about careers, and strategy-oriented resumes, cover letters, and interviewing techniques to prepare and help you get out of an unhappy work situation. Some career counselors work exclusively with lawyers. Most have graduate degrees in counseling, education, or law, and fall into any of the following categories.

1. Career counselors who work primarily with lawyers. Ask a local law school or local Bar Association for referrals.

2. Career counselors at law schools. Call the law school you attended for information. Nearly all have free or low-cost career counseling for their alumni through the school's Office of Career Development or Office of Career Services.

3. Career counseling groups/workshops.

If counseling isn't your thing, then you may want to check out the resources available through one of the following:

1. Wishcraft groups. Group "brainstorming" on a regular basis, see the book *Wishcraft* by Barbara Sher (listed in the resource section) for more information.

2. Bar associations. Most state, city, and local bar associations sponsor many excellent career workshops for lawyers. Contact your local bar for information.

3. The Five O'Clock Club. Group counseling/strategy meetings for executives of all types. Main location in mid-Manhattan, other chapters have been forming all around the country. Started by well-known career coach/author Kate Wendleton. In New York, call: (212) 286-4500. Located at 300 E. 40th St., New York, NY 10016

PSYCHOLOGICAL COUNSELING

There are all kinds of therapy, both short- and long-term, that can help you gain greater self-awareness and can help you get "unstuck" if you feel unhappy but immobilized. Believe me, you are not alone. As one therapist recently told me, "Half my patients are lawyers."

There are even psychologists who specialize in working with lawyers. In the meantime, there are some definite warning signs that you're unhappiness might be giving you lead feet:

- Significant change in appetite, weight loss or weight gain

- Major change in sleep patterns

- Loss of energy or fatigue

- Feelings of worthlessness or excessive feelings of guilt

- Diminished interest in or loss of pleasure in usual activities and/or relationships

- Inability to concentrate or make decisions

PRO BONO AND PART-TIME WORK

Like the other suggestions in this chapter, pro bono (volunteer legal) work offers you a chance to explore a new area without making any drastic decisions. For example, if you feel that moving into a different practice area could make you happier, pro bono work is a good way to try it out before committing. Also, it is an opportunity to get experience in another field and thus more ammunition for your resume.

Even though you are doing the work for nonprofit organizations, it does not mean that you cannot use it to gain experience in a practice area, such as matrimonial law or real estate, that is practiced in the private sector. If, for example, you have an interest in moving from commercial litigation to family law, there are many opportunities to become trained in and execute no-contest divorces for people who cannot afford a lawyer. Now, you have some experience in divorce law on your resume plus you have met people in the field of family law to network with. (Not to mention the good deed you have done).

If instead you want to try a career move from the private to the public sector, you should know from reading chapter 1 that public sector lawyers report among the greatest levels of satisfaction within the practice of law. You may find that you are much happier in the nonprofit end of law where you: (1) can help "real live" people, instead of corporations; (2) have a high level of responsibility and client interaction; and (3) work in an environment that may be less stuffy than a law firm.

You may also discover that getting involved in pro bono work while remaining a full-time, practicing lawyer may make you feel much better about your life right away. Then, as you gain more pro bono experience, you can decide if you want to move into it as a full-time venture. If you are one of those people who went to law school to "do good," and feel that the practice of law has left you feeling empty inside, you may be very happy in the nonprofit world.

Performing pro bono work on a part-time, volunteer basis, in order to get into the field full-time, is a very effective method of demonstrating a commitment to the field and making contacts in that field. The single most often cited factor for nonprofit employers in making hiring decisions is "a demonstrated commitment" to nonprofit work. The field also operates primarily on contacts, not public advertisements for positions.

You can sign up for pro bono work through the American Bar Association (ABA), or your state or local bar association program. The ABA publishes a nationwide directory of pro bono programs, which includes all state and city bar association pro bono programs, including contact names and numbers. You can obtain it by calling the ABA Publications Department at (800) 285-2221 (Item # 4297000, $15.00). It's an excellent resource. Just browsing through the directory can give you ideas of other types/areas of practice, in addition to giving you pro bono information.

You should also know about the National Lawyers Guild if you are considering a move to the public sector. It is the nation's largest and oldest public-interest law organization, with chapters all over the country. The organization is involved in promoting social change through legal forums, publications, and committee work. It is also an excellent way to meet people and to network; plus, they publish a newsletter containing public sector job listings. For more information, write: National Lawyers Guild, New York City Chapter, 55 Avenue of the Americas, New York, NY 10013-1698.

State and local bar associations also have extensive pro bono directories, containing information about opportunities offered through their own organization and opportunities offered through area organizations, such as the Public Defender. For a summary of all of the pro bono opportunities offered through the Association of the Bar of the City of New York see the Appendix on p. 159. I included it, even though I know you may not live in New York, to show you the breadth of opportunities available to you. It's a great source of ideas, as well as pro bono experience. You can expect your state/local bar to have a similar (though perhaps shorter) list.

FURTHERING YOUR EDUCATION: SWITCHING GEARS

Like pro bono work, enhancing your academic credentials is a good way to experiment with another field and to build your resume. More schoolwork? After all of those years of law school, plus the bar exam? No, I am not suggesting you go to medical school or obtain a Ph.D. There are some short, easy ways to credential yourself in another field.

For example, many attorneys want to transition out of law into business. As a substitute for business experience, they take some courses and add them to their resume. Many MBAs offer certificate programs, where you can take fewer courses and qualify for a certificate in one, specific area of business. Continuing Education courses offered through major universities also have certificate programs.

One litigation attorney took a real estate management course from NYU. He liked it, got to know his professor, and later became a real estate attorney. Another lawyer working for the federal government took a magazine editorial course and shortly thereafter started working at a magazine, through meeting a guest speaker at the course. She is now a magazine editor.

So, not only do you get some course credits, but you get to meet professors and classmates, who are already in the field in which you are interested. Now you have networking opportunities in addition to knowledge. You might find out about associations you can join or newsletters in that field that contain job listings. You also have demonstrated a serious interest in the new field to future employers. You have indicated your commitment and your willingness to learn, and you are more likely to get an interview and get hired.

You can use this method either to switch gears within the law (litigator to real estate attorney), or to leave law entirely (real estate attorney to commercial real estate broker). It's a good first step out of whatever field/specialty you are stuck in right now. CLE (continuing legal education) courses offered by bar associations nationwide are obviously a good route to go as well if your first goal is to switch specialty areas within the practice of law.

OTHER DEGREES LAWYERS HAVE SOUGHT

Sometimes people do have the desire to get a full degree. Larry Richard, profiled in this book, now has a Ph.D. in psychology. Another lawyer recently obtained a master's in social work to help her in her new career in public policy. Often, if it is a full degree, people enroll in a master's program, which usually takes two years full-time, three to five years part-time.

Below are a few suggestions for some master's programs that you may not have considered yet:

- Masters in Psychology

- Masters in Education

- Masters in Journalism/Communications

- Masters in Business Administration

- Masters in Social Work

- Masters In Public Policy

- Degree programs designed for mid-career changers (i.e., Harvard's JFK School of Government mid-career program in public policy, and Princeton's Woodrow Wilson School).

And if a several-year commitment isn't in the cards for you, here are two summer programs that might be more easily fit into you calender:

- Radcliff University Publishing Course

  Lind Hess, Director
  6 Ash Street
  Cambridge, MA 02138
  (617) 494-2333

- New York University (summer programs offered in journalism and nonprofit organization, among others)

  Office of Summer Sessions
  22 Washington Square N.
  New York, NY 10011
  (212) 998-4500
  website—http://www.nyu.edu

TEMPING AS A LAWYER: ALTERNATIVE FOR THE '90S

In the 1990s, the formerly stuffy, conservative practice of law became revolutionized. Temporary, or "Temp" lawyers are not only accepted as a viable alternative to associates, but they are very much in demand. Lesley Friedman (profiled in this book), who started one of the first temp agencies for lawyers, saw her business mushroom in the nine years that she owned it, which spanned the mid-80s to the mid 90s. Now, temporary agencies for lawyers are popping up all over the country. Cost has been a major factor in this development—law firms have found it very cost effective to hire temps to handle overflow work, allowing firms to conservatively monitor permanent hiring.

What does this mean for you? Well, it can open up your options. If you have the credentials temp agencies for lawyers are looking for—good academic standing in law school, large law-firm experience, and experience in a "hot" practice area, such as patent law—you will be in demand for temp work. So, if you want to have more time and flexibility, temping may be for you. It's a great way to see if you really want to pursue another line of work, and the money is often quite good.

Even though your hours during temporary projects may be long, you can space out your assignments over the year. You will also be relieved of the pressure of rainmaking or struggling to stay on partnership track. This will give you some space to explore, and perhaps start a new career, while still being able to pay your bills. Or, you might find that the lifestyle of "permanently" temping really suits you. See the classified ads under "Attorney" or "Law" for names of temporary agencies for attorneys in your area.

OTHER ALTERNATIVE WORK ARRANGEMENTS FOR THE '90S

TELECOMMUTING

Telecommuting is a way for an attorney to work from home and fax or modem work to the office. Telecommuting may not cut down on the number of billable hours, but it can provide other benefits for lawyers. Increased flexibility and greater access to family members, for instance. Reduced stress, no commute, and a relaxed wardrobe are other benefits. And, like in the sabbatical section above, believe it or not, it has been done by lawyers!

MOONLIGHTING: DUAL-CAREER LAWYERS

Some lawyers decide to permanently mix the practice of law with a long-term hobby or interest. They have decided not to leave the practice of law, whether for financial reasons or because they like practicing. So they practice law by day, and are writers, dancers, musicians, and actors by night. Some, like Debevoise & Plimpton's Louis Begely, a well-known writer, end up working a twenty-hour day. Others find less time-consuming day jobs. A clinical professor at a New-York-area law school, for example, teaches by day, and has another career as an actor in television, commercials, and off–Broadway. These lawyers have reconciled law practice and their creative interests by managing to do both.

PART-TIME WORK

Many law firms have formal part-time work policies, but in actuality, few of their attorneys have utilized them. In the world of law firms, part-time work can mean a forty- to fifty-hour work week. However, as alternative work arrangements have become a part of the workforce, law firms have adapted to some extent. Part-timers have adapted as well. "The key is to have some flexibility," said one. "You have to be able to take calls from the client on your day off or stay late for a court arraignment," she said.

Women Lawyers:
A Special Case

BIRDS OF A FEATHER

Almost all of my female friends are lawyers. Ten years out of law school, however, almost none of them are practicing attorneys anymore. Like myself, they attended law school as a way to continue their academic and personal success. During school, there were the usual moans and groans about heavy workloads and demanding professors, but we all started our legal careers with the eagerness typical of greenhorns.

The transition from learning about law to actually practicing it was, to say the least, challenging. Making the change from reading hypotheticals in casebooks to actually handling real clients was as exciting as it promised to be. During that first year, there really were no noticeable differences in treatment between us and our male peers. It was somewhere after the second year that the paths began to diverge.

Of my friends that married and began planning families, many of them found it difficult to balance the demands of practicing law with having children. Some claimed it was the nature of the work itself; others said they received a less-than-supportive attitude from the partners at their firms; still others reported a combination of both the former and the latter. Some of my other female friends simply realized they hated practicing law—it was tedious, uncreative, and left zero time for a life outside of work. In addition, as they progressed, these women began to get the feeling they were not valued as much as men by their superiors. The partners in many of these firms (who tend to be primarily male) spent more time grooming their male associates for future partner slots in typical male-bonding fashion: drinks, golfing expeditions, etc.

Percent of Female Law School Graduates, Nationwide

Approximately 43 percent of all law school graduates are female, almost half of law school classes.

What happened to these women following their respective rude-awakening bumps on the head courtesy of the legal glass ceiling? Alternatives to careers in law became sought after options. I myself became a career counselor. Of my core group of friends, one became a vice-president in a bank; one left a senior level position at a government agency to take an entry-level career in advertising; another went back to school for a masters in teaching and later become a high-school English teacher; one became a writer. Now, at the age that we would rightly expect to be making partner, not one of us is still in traditional law practice.

Number of Women Lawyers

Women constitute approximately 23 percent of all lawyers, and are approximately 207,738 in number.

(According to the ABA Commission on Women in the Profession report, 1995)

From what I've seen in my professional life, my friends were not unusual. In my seven years as a career counselor for law students and lawyers, I have seen this pattern over and over, and it isn't a regional phenomenon. It's the same everywhere. Overall dissatisfaction among women in the legal profession is especially high. The rate of dissatisfaction for female attorneys in private practice rose from 29 to 41 percent from 1984 to 1990, according to an American Bar Association Study conducted in 1990. The rate for male attorneys during the same years rose much less significantly, from 14 to 28 percent.

A Long Way to Go, Baby

In the nation's 250 largest law firms, 13.6 percent of the partners are women; about 50 percent are non-equity partners.

(According to the *National Law Journal* Study of women and minorities at the largest 250 firms in the country)

What does this indicate about women in the legal profession? It appears that the playing ground is level during law school (with women now enrolling in numbers almost equal to men), but some time after the first few years of practice, the picture begins to change.

THE POST-GRAD BLUES

There appears to be another big discrepancy between male and female lawyers. In a nutshell, male lawyers make more money:

- In a 1995 survey of young lawyers by the ABA, the median annual salary for the male respondents was $50,000–$59,000—for the females it was $40,000–$49,000.

- In a 1995 survey conducted by *Working Woman* magazine, annual earnings for women lawyers averaged $47,684, compared to an average of $64,324 for men.

- A 1994 Price Waterhouse survey reported that male attorneys holding the position of general counsel make 19 percent more than their female counterparts.

Perhaps the most disheartening numbers (and to me the most shocking) involve the very small number of female partners that exist. A Connecticut Bar Association study in 1994 reported that men who are partners in firms make, on average, about $23,000 a year more than female partners. In the corporate world, female lawyers earn, on average, about $15,500 less per year than their male counterparts.

There are also a disproportionate number of female partners who are non-equity partners. This was confirmed in a *National Law Journal* survey of women and minorities at the nation's 250 largest law firms. Female partnership constitutes 13.6 percent of all law partners, but only about half have equity (ownership, or share of the partnership profits, as opposed to salary). Non-equity partnerships have become commonplace in recent years. For example, according to that same *National Law Journal* survey, the firm with the highest number of female partners is Reid & Priest, with 39.7 percent. However, 22 of the 31 female partners, or 71 percent, are non-equity partners.

DISSATISFACTION LEVELS FOR WOMEN IN LAW

Almost twice as many women then men in private practice are dissatisfied, reporting that they continue to experience a far more negative work environment than men as lawyers. Here are some of the reported reasons:

- More women report that they don't have the opportunity to advance (30 percent vs. 21 percent) and that advancement is not determined by the quality of one's work (32 percent vs. 24 percent)

- More women report that they are not respected and treated as professional colleagues by their superiors (13 percent vs. 7 percent)

- Women continue to be far worse off financially than their male colleagues in most positions

- Fewer women are partners (only 18 percent of the female respondents, compared to 45 percent of the men)

(*Source:* The State of the Legal Professions study, 1990 A.B.A. Sample of lawyers of all ages)

WHY DON'T WOMEN MAKE PARTNER?

Aside from any inherent prejudices against women, according to *The New York Times* ("Women Striving to Make it Rain at Law Firms," May 21, 1996), women do not bring in the "rain" (i.e., business) as much as the men do. Why not? According to the article, women rarely partake, or have an opportunity to partake, in sports or other so-called "male bonding" activities; have more family pressures that prevent them from doing a lot of entertaining or business travel; are not, in general, confrontational enough for litigation careers; or do not like confrontation all together.

These women also claimed to not be in the best position to woo the "plum" clients of law firms: major corporations (which are still controlled primarily by men). In fact, a recent census conducted by Catalyst, a nonprofit women's research group reported that women hold just about 2 percent of the power positions in corporate America. And of the nation's 500 largest companies, only 61 have a woman among their five top earners, or have a quarter or more of their officers who are women. The American Corporate Counsel Association has over 10,000 members; slightly less than 3,000 were women at last count.

So what can you do? Of the women who are partners at major New York firms right now, many have succeeded by finding powerful mentors—both male and female—or by prac-

Organizations For Women Attorneys To Get Involved In:

- American Bar Association Law Practice Management Section—Women Rainmaker's Interest Group (there are also other areas within the A.B.A. that are involved with women lawyers, such as the A.B.A. Commission on Women).
- The Women's Campaign Fund
- National Association of Women Business Owners
- State and local Bar Association Women's Bars, Sections, and Committees (virtually every state has one).

(Source: *The New York Times*, May 21, 1996)

ticing in non-litigation areas such as trusts and estates, labor law, real estate, matrimonial law. But there are other, simple things you can do, too:

- Answer your own phone
- Call your clients regularly (even if you have no business reason, just to say hello)
- Go out to lunch
- Network with people very senior and very junior to you (the junior people will remember the people who were kind to them)

WOMEN WHO HAVE LEFT THE PRACTICE OF LAW

Given all of the above, it is no wonder that some women have decided to leave the practice of law. In fact, of the 719 associates who started working at five of the top-grossing law firms in 1987, almost all of the women—a staggering 94 percent—have left their jobs, compared to 72 percent of the men (*New York Magazine*, December 11, 1995), The vast majority of female hires left big firms after several years, even before partnership was a confirmed no.

Martha Fay Africa, partner in the recruitment firm Major, Hagen and Africa, and chair of the ABA Glass Ceiling Task Force, calls the 50 percent of women lawyers who leave private practice within five years of starting "Darwin's daughters." According to Africa, "They leave to better ensure survival for themselves and their children. It is survival of the fittest...the people who survive are the people who leave. They are...leading full and satisfying lives."

Africa believes that the large law firms have no incentive to change because of the market forces of supply and demand. "Law firms are quite secure at the entry level," she said. "They have a steady stream of people." Africa goes on to say that, at upper levels, women have sometimes been able to craft situations that work in small law firms or have left for in-house counsel positions in Corporate America.

IT'S A BIG BOAT—AND WE'RE ALL IN IT

Although there's a high degree of dissatisfaction for women lawyers, it doesn't seem to be a phenomenon of the legal profession. In fact, women lawyers seem to have commonalities with most women holding executive positions. A *Fortune* magazine study in September of 1995 reported that, 300 career women, ages 35 to 49, had considered the following:

Sample Number of Female Partners at Major New York City Law Firms:

Sullivan & Cromwell:
Women: 6, Men: 103

Skadden Arps Slate Meagher & Flom:
Women: 22, Men: 102

Davis Polk & Wardwell:
Women: 12, Men: 92

Dewey Ballantine:
Women: 4, Men: 68

Source: National Association for Law Placement Directory of Legal Employers, 1995.

Starting a business:	45%
Changing jobs in same career:	44%
Going back to school:	38%
Taking a sabbatical:	37%
Changing careers:	35%
Leaving job and not working:	31%

Of course, not all of the reasons here are completely unique to women. Men who leave the legal profession cite many of the same motivations as women: the "up-or-out" mentality, the long hours, the endless confrontation of litigation. The law is no longer a profession today but a " business."

But there are some particular complaints I hear over and over from women lawyers, some of the most common being:

- Hated the fighting inherent in litigation
- Wanted to do "good things" for people

- Conscious decision to have a more "balanced" life

- Wanted to spend time with family

- Wanted to get away from the "sweatshop mentality" of today's law firms

- Had to hide, or lie about, child rearing and/or family–related activities (including in at least one case, the fact that the lawyer had children at all)

- Dislike of office politics/frustration over lack of possibility of forming good relationships, lack of bonding. Not invited to participate in social and networking opportunities, such as going out for drinks after work

This isn't to say that all is lost. The future for women lawyers, and for those who choose not to practice, actually looks very good. Several societal and economic indicators point toward a hopeful future.

There is a major trend in both the private and the public sector toward mediation and arbitration instead of litigation. Alternatives to traditional litigation—the field now called alternative dispute resolution—is becoming more popular. Another hot area of law emerging right now is elder law, due to the problems inherent in an increasingly aging population. Female attorneys appear to be taking this area by storm, occupying about 40 percent of The Academy of Elder Lawyers legal staff. Another growing area, intellectual property, boasts a high percentage of female lawyers who are copyright attorneys—40 percent are female. And finally, employment law also reports a high percentage of female attorneys among its ranks.

Honorable?

Approximately 12 percent of the federal judiciary is comprised of female judges.

Women are continuing to be a major force in the practice of law at all levels, despite the apparent obstacles. It appears that women are continuing to enroll in law school in very large numbers. According to the Law School Admissions Counsel Law Services Report, women make up nearly half of the national law student population. In 1996, the female applicant pool was approximately 46 percent.

Additionally, female lawyers are better equipped now to do the all-important "power networking" necessary to obtain clients. With more women obtaining high-level positions (such as corporate counsel jobs), the "boys clubs" that were once off limits are now going coed, leading to more business opportunities for women in general. According to the 1995 ABA study on women in the legal profession, the number of women in senior-level corporate counsel positions is increasing between 3 and 5 percent annually.

Where's the proof? Turn to chapter 6 and read about Lesley Friedman and Carol Kanarek, who have made a niche for themselves in business and have had very lucrative careers. At the highest levels, women are succeeding as well. Let's not forget that two women—Ruth Bader Ginsberg and Sandra Day O'Connor—are Supreme Court Justices, not to mention Attorney General Janet Reno. And let's not forget about Hillary Clinton—another successful female attorney who is certainly blowing some of those old first lady stereotypes out of the water.

THE POWER BROKERS

In addition to specialty areas of practice, the general business climate also seems to be favoring women right now. The number of woman-owned businesses surged 43 percent between 1987 and 1992, according to a Census Bureau study. Women now own more than six million businesses in the United States—far outpacing the male entrepreneurial counterparts. Other end-of-the-century phenomenons are the trends toward setting up shop at home and working on a project-by-project basis instead of on a full-time basis. With the prices of PCs, e-mail, fax machines, and other office equipment coming down to the average consumer's level, there's less and less reason to schlep across hill and dale (or pavement and toll plazas, as it were).

So, the seemingly unusual career paths that my friends have chosen, have turned out to be not so unusual in the final analysis. For many reasons—some specifically related to the practice of law and some related to general societal and economic factors—some women are choosing not to stay in the practice of law. It is disappointing that one of the professions in which women were thought to have made the greatest strides and have the most opportunities has the same setbacks that women have struggled to overcome for centuries. But there is certainly no reason to throw in the towel if you truly love practicing. Law is still a very high paying profession with much opportunity—tapped and untapped. Your job is to figure out if it is, in fact, the right profession for you.

Profiles

Lori Vendinello: From Lawyer to Director of a Bicycle Tour Company

Non-Legal Career: Director, La Corsa Tours, Company That Leads Groups on Bicycle Tours through Italy and France

Year Graduated From Law School: 1986

Years Practicing Law: Approximately Seven

I knew that Lori was not your typical lawyer when we decided where to meet for the interview: She said we would have to go somewhere where she could lock up her bike. Lori described herself as having mid-back length blondish hair, a black bike, and carrying a black Saucony workout bag. Obviously, this was not someone rushing to meet me after a long day on Wall Street.

Early for our interview, I scouted the coffee bar where we were to meet, scanning the crowd for an athletic looking person. But every female with blond hair that was alone was carrying a very chic looking black bag or briefcase, and no one had a bike with them. But when Lori appeared, she was immediately recognizable—she looked *healthy*, tan, and refreshed. She definitely stood out from the ashen, weary New York City crowd.

As we sat down, she showed me the brochure for her company. "Do you wonder if a 'challenging' bike vacation is for you?" questions the La Corsa Tours brochure. "Four hundred beautiful miles later...the answer will be emphatically 'yes!' For an exhilarating vacation in a fabulous setting with...attentive personal service and food to-die-for, we invite you to join us on a La Corsa tour."

Sound inviting to all you lawyers out there staring out at the setting sun from a forty-floor office tower? I would venture to guess that it does. For Lori, it has been her life for the past three years since she and her husband started La Corsa Tours.

How did this Law Review student who loved law school make such a dramatic break from practicing law? Lori, a 1986 Boston University Law School graduate, had what most law students dream about. Stellar grades that put her in the top 10 percent of her class and a job offer from a very prestigious law firm. In fact, Lori was the first B.U. graduate to be hired by the firm. "I loved law school," she said. "I went to the firm because I wanted to be a ground breaker for my school." On the heels of a two-year federal clerkship, and an MBA in corporate finance obtained while she was clerking, Lori started work at the firm with a lot of confidence.

It ebbed quickly. "It was demoralizing," she said. " It wasn't the hours, it was the lack of control and the inconsiderate treatment by senior associates and partners. I bought my apartment, paid off my loans, and got the hell out!"

In addition, Lori cited lack of guidance and mentoring, as well as the feeling of isolation she had because she was the only B.U. person at the firm. "It was very clubby," she remembered. Three years later, she left for what many associates choose, an in-house corporate counsel position. Lori got a job in-house at AT&T in Basking Ridge, New Jersey. Although she liked the work and the greater degree of responsibility she was given, the corporate culture and the one-and-a-half-hour commute each way from New York City wore her out. "I would say thank you to God for sending me back to civilization every night when I would finally see the New York City skyline."

She eventually transferred to the Manhattan office but found it to be "analogous to committing career suicide." Outside of the main legal department, there was not much action. Part

Lawyer as Travel Tour Director:

Adavantages:
- dream job that most people fantasize about
- travel
- autonomy
- outdoor work

Disadvantages:
- work is physically difficult
- not as much intellectual stimulation as practicing law
- financial uncertainty

of her job involved rubber stamping documents with a stamp marked "approved by legal department"—she lasted two years.

In the summer of 1992 while still with AT&T, Lori went on a bicycling vacation in Italy sponsored by an American company. She had always been a great athlete, and she was training for a triathlon at the time. Although she started out as a runner, she found that her best times in triathlons were in bicycling. The trip to Italy, in addition to a vacation, was intended to help her train.

Although she enjoyed the tour, she didn't find it challenging or particularly well-organized. "I could do a much better job," she remembered telling her husband. This was the moment that sparked the idea for her business. When she returned to the states, she organized a tour on a volunteer basis for the New York Cycle Club. She was still at AT&T, but with five weeks vacation had time to start organizing trips.

In 1993, Lori and her husband took their first commercial trip, and incorporated La Corsa. Her husband co-directed the company with her, but kept his day job as an accountant in the financial industry. He still works full-time.

Since 1993, the company has grown to eight trips a year, offering challenging tours to advanced bicyclists. "That is our market niche, and [it] distinguishes us from other companies," she said. They also try to incorporate some extra adventure into the tours by taking vacationers to undiscovered parts of Italy and France.

What are the disadvantages? Well, in Lori's case the disadvantages are also the advantages. For example, clothes. "This is dressed up for me," she said at the interview, looking down at her tank top and wrap skirt. Although she loves her life, she feels "left out sometimes" when she has lunch with friends on Wall Street. "I am no longer a part of that world." She has to be physically in great shape and rides 100 miles a day. She gripes about having to work out so much. But you can tell that she is enjoying it and very proud of herself. Lori has also had to learn to speak Italian fluently. Again, it is something that was hard work but well worth it.

She also misses the security and benefits that come with working for a large organization. In fact, she originally used the coffeehouse in which we met for the interview as her first La Corsa office, organizing the company over café lattes. Despite the disadvantages she is content. "I would never go back to working for anyone else again."

Lori uses her marketing skills to publicize the company and to attract clients. She often uses her legal skills in making contracts with vendors, hotels, and liability insurance companies—a big concern for travel companies such as La Corsa.

Lawyers who are entrepreneurs, like Lori, are often very happy. They are used to hard work and pressure but really love the fact that all of the hard work is now going for something all their own—not to the partners, firms, or clients. They often make very good business people.

In Lori's case, business satisfies her desire to work independently. She is different from most lawyers who leave in that she adored law school. But what does it say about the legal profession that someone who loved law school hated practicing so much that left the profession? Lori is still obviously a high achiever and would be impressive in any field. However, the legal profession really lost out when it lost Lori.

LAWRENCE OTIS GRAHAM: RENAISSANCE MAN

Alternative Legal Career: Author, Television Personality, Speaker, President, Progressive Management Associates

Year Graduated From Law School: 1988

Law School Attended: Harvard

Years Practicing Law: Five

Lawrence Otis Graham has always loved to write. So much, in fact, that he has published eleven books by the age of thirty-three, the first of which was published when he was an undergraduate at Princeton. So it is no surprise that one of his articles, "Invisible Man," made the cover of *New York* magazine in 1992, and made Graham famous at the age of twenty-nine.

The story of his experience as a Harvard-educated black lawyer who went undercover as a busboy at an all-white Greenwich, Connecticut country club (proving it to be as discriminatory as he feared) garnered national attention. The *New York* magazine story caught the eye of national and international press, and is now being made into a major feature film by Warner Bros., starring Denzel Washington as Graham.

At the time he went undercover, he was a third-year law student and was researching his book called *The Best Companies for Minorities*. "Writing is my hobby," he said. "By the time I was in law school I had already published seven or eight books." He obtained his first publisher and agent when he was a college student, by taking the bus one day into New York City from Princeton and making cold calls from the yellow pages at a pay phone on Park Avenue. "I was naively optimistic," he recalls. One of the last literary agent entries in the yellow pages, Susan Zeckendorf, agreed to represent him and became his first literary agent.

Despite his early literary success, he had always wanted to be a lawyer, so he attended Harvard Law School after graduating from Princeton. Graham was still researching and writing his seventh book when he started his legal career as a corporate associate at New York's Weil, Gotshal, & Manges. "I loved it—I'm an entrepreneurial person, and I found the corporate aspect fascinating." Not surprisingly, he also liked the writing and drafting part of law practice.

But his experience as a young black lawyer was mixed. He was disheartened to find that racism existed even in the upper echelons of large law firms and corporations. "Weil Gotshal was great— it's a very liberal-minded firm, but other firms I had interviewed with had either not hired, or could not retain minority attorneys." What he found most unsettling was the inability of minority attorneys to find mentors and crucial networking opportunities that other lawyers found playing golf, on the tennis court, or at private clubs.

"In 1992, people were amazed that Ivy League graduates earning $500,000 could not get into country clubs." His own experience going undercover at a country club was so shocking that he decided to send his story into *New York* magazine. They thought it was so explosive they decided to make it their cover story. Graham was somewhat surprised by the immense response.

What You Should Learn from Graham:

His chief advice to those seeking non-legal careers: (1) Find great mentors who really believe in you, (2) get on the board of an organization that has nothing to do with lawyers, but where a lawyer would be needed (i.e., NOW, NAACP, UJA, or even a local community organization, like the Neighborhood Housing Services (NHS)), and (3) do research to find out about non-legal positions by reading publications, such as *Current Biography*.

"To me, it was such an apparent issue...I grew up seeing other kids get out of the pool at swim clubs when I jumped in, either that or their parents would pull them out of the pool." he said. " But it resonated for the public." The reaction was enormous.

Two days after the article appeared, Hollywood called. His secretary came into Graham's office looking perplexed. She told him that Paramount Pictures was on the phone and wanted to make a movie of his story, starring Eddie Murphy. "It's a crank call," he told her. "Hang up." After Twentieth Century Fox called with a similar proposal (only this time starring Wesley Snipes) he hung up again. Finally, when Warner Brothers called, he took a message to be sure the number was bona fide, and called them back. The story was eventually sold to them at an auction for $300,000, a record for a magazine story being sold to Hollywood at that time.

By this point, Graham's focus changed. "I had always defined myself as a full-time attorney who wrote in my spare time...there was never a time when I did not see myself as a lawyer," he said. But offer after offer from publishers piled in. He realized that the opportunities to write were too good to pass up and accepted a two-book contract deal from Harper Collins and left full-time law practice.

He remained of counsel to a law firm but spent most of his time writing and on the lecture circuit. Making the transition was not a struggle. He had established himself enough so that he was actually earning more from his writing than from his six-figure salary as a lawyer. But it was the fact that he was a lawyer that made him write the story that made him famous.

Although Graham's story is perhaps unusual for a typical associate, his desire to combine an interest in law, writing, and social issues is not. He just managed to put it all together in an unbelievably successful way. Following his departure from full-time practice Graham continued to write. His works include *Member of the Club*, a series of twelve essays on his experiences as a young black professional. He also wrote another cover story for *New York* magazine, this time writing about his experiences living in Harlem for a month.

He also continued to work for social change, both in the legal and corporate worlds. He opened a diversity consulting practice in 1991, working with law firms and corporations including Kraft, Hewlett Packard and Blue Cross/Blue Shield, advising them on workforce diversity issues. He now spends about half of his time consulting and the other half writing and speaking. He is a frequent television guest, appearing on CNN, the Comedy Channel's *Politically Incorrect* with Bill Maher, as well as *Oprah*, *Donahue*, and other talk shows. He is also an adjunct professor at Fordham University.

If this all weren't enough, in spring 1997 Graham is slated to become a talk show host himself. *Lawrence & Betsy: Black & White*, to be nationally syndicated, will feature Graham with Betsy Hart, a Caucasian conservative Republican professor, in a kind of "He Said, She Said" political/racial venture. The two often speak together and plan to co-author a book.

Despite his own choice, Graham does not regret his experience as a lawyer, and in fact strongly recommends that graduates practice law for a few years before leaving. "If I had not gone to Weil, Gotshal, I would not have an appreciation for how people get things done in a very organized, competent manner...in very few industries are there people as smart and as excellent as in law firm practice. I am totally grateful for that experience, and I am very, very fortunate."

Throughout the interview, Graham repeated that he has been extremely fortunate throughout his career. Fortunate, perhaps, but ambitious, talented, and passionate about his work—without a doubt.

GLENN GULINO: FROM LAWYER TO TALENT AGENT

Alternative Legal Career: Agent, the William Morris Agency, Inc.

Year Graduated From Law School: 1989

Law School Attended: Boston College

Number of Years in Practice Before Leaving: Approximately Four

Glenn Gulino does not look like a typical lawyer. He breezes into our interview with his sunglasses on, dressed in a black Hugo Boss suit with black and white polka dot suspenders, radiating energy and charisma. It is August, and he has just returned from the Cannes Film Festival. Indeed, Glenn is not a lawyer any more—he is now an agent with William Morris, the oldest and most prestigious talent agency in the world.

The road to William Morris was not, as many lawyers might think, an easy one. Glenn started to work on making entertainment-related contacts back in high school when he was in a band and hung out with musicians. After deciding that he would rather represent rock stars than try to become one, Glenn attended Boston College Law School. While there, he started the Arts, Entertainment and Sports Law Society. He also started to network with other entertainment lawyers by attending entertainment law symposia and conferences. Right away, Glenn caught on to the credo of the entertainment world: "It's not what you know, but who you know," and became a master at networking.

While in law school he was also able to do an externship with an entertainment law firm in Boston that represented the musical group New Kids on the Block. They offered Glenn a job, but, needing to make some money, he went with a larger law firm instead. He became an associate in the corporate public finance department of Mudge, Rose, Guthrie, Alexander & Ferdon for two years before joining LeBoeuf, Lamb in New York. He sensed right away that it wasn't for him and started looking for an entertainment law job.

"I would go to California on assignment, and take extra days to attend things at the Century City Bar Association and the Beverly Hills Bar Association. I went to everything," he remembers. Glenn was quite savvy about the keys to networking—asking people for advice, information, and referrals—but not directly for a job." I was looking to get out of this drudgery, but I knew enough not to ask, "Can you give me a job?'"

"The day I came to New York in 1989, I joined every entertainment organization imaginable," he said. He also started attending entertainment law section meetings at the New York State Bar, and the American Bar Association. He learned a lot by reading the entertainment trades—*Billboard, Variety,* the *Hollywood Reporter*—on a regular basis. He knew that it would take immense social skills, time, and hard work to break into the industry. "It takes a lot of phone calls and a lot of energy."

In 1993 he decided to quit his six figure salary job at LeBoeuf cold turkey. "My heart is in the entertainment business," he told the partners. "A lot of my

Glenn's Advice to Lawyers Interested in the Entertainment Industry:

- Networking pays off
- When networking, give the others a chance to tell their story. Ask for advice and names of more contacts to network with—but never ask for a job.
- Do your research— read all the trade papers on a regular basis
- Be prepared to give it time
- Determine what it is you like about the entertainment industry. If you like the process, for example, try producing
- You have to have a sincere interest in the business and a strong work ethic to succeed. In a business full of @!#*!, character and sincerity are key!

friends were surprised I had the guts to do it." He had saved some money from LeBoeuf, and once again headed west to L.A., where he started cold calling agents in the Hollywood Creative Directory. Glenn thought he might like to be an agent because of his interpersonal skills, and because, unlike law, it is a "proactive, not reactive" career.

One of the agencies he cold-called back in New York City, Fifi Oscard, said to "come right over," and hired him for a $180-dollar-a-week, low-level position—obviously, a pretty substantial paycut from his days at LeBoeuf. A few months later, that job led to an interview for a job in the mailroom at the William Morris Agency.

He had to meet with seven agents just to get a starting position at the bottom of the barrel. "Barry Diller started in the mailroom there, David Geffen started there," he said. Like most jobs in the entertainment industry, in order to move up you have to pay your dues. William Morris has a five-year training program for people who want to become agents, but the equivalent of being a first-year associate there was to work in the mailroom and run scripts around town for agents.

"It was the winter of '93, and I was in snow up to my ankles doing errands," Glenn remembers. He was thirty at the time. His starting salary was $300 a week, better than at Fifi Oscard, but a long cry from his salary as a lawyer. The usual path was to become "king or queen of the mailroom," then become a floater who temped for different agents. Eventually, if things worked out, you could become an assistant to a particular agent in a particular department of interest, like Motion Pictures or Music. Then, after some time of training, you would get promoted to a full agent. Two years into the five-year training program, Glenn made agent.

He advanced more quickly in part because of a controversial article featuring him entitled: "Michael Ovitz Michael Ovitz Michael Ovitz; The Mogul Wannabes at the William Morris Agency Must First Have to Wannabe in the Mailroom" in *The New York Times*, which was also picked up by international papers and appeared all over the world. Although Glenn had no idea he would be the feature of the article (the reporter had interviewed a dozen people), he apparently represented a unique slant, as a former lawyer working in the mailroom. It received a mixed reaction, internally, but after it appeared, everyone in the agency knew who he was.

When Glenn became a full agent, he was able to represent clients of the William Morris Agency, which is analogous to making partner at a law firm, at least from the status angle, if not financially. He was assigned to a new division, Licensing and Merchandising. He now primarily works on projects involving signature lines for celebrities—for example, if a celebrity wanted to start his own clothing line, Glenn would help put the deal together.

Glenn's new career uses his legal skills nicely: It involves business skills, interpreting contractual agreements, intellectual property rights, research skills, as well as gathering information on different companies and studying their annual reports. Good negotiation skills are also paramount. Although he has been an agent for a relatively short time, so far it is a good fit for Glenn.

It is a tough job in terms of dealing with clients, just as it is for lawyers. "We are a buffer to the client," Glenn said. "We are dealing with people's feelings and we need to be as careful as possible." Although he is making considerably less than he would have had he remained at the firm, the potential to make money as an agent is much greater in the long run. For example, an agent could make a piece of the overall business he brings into the company.

"Agents are creative in a non-linear way," he said. "Lawyers are always reactive—fixing problems—it's very refreshing to do something proactive instead." But there are negatives as well. "While lawyers are respected for their intellect, agents sometimes rule by fear. It can be a swimming with sharks environment." Like almost everything in the entertainment world, the competition is fierce.

For now, he is grateful for the experience of working for William Morris, which worldwide, has 200 plus agents, and a lot of clout. "I am very fortunate to be able to learn from them," he said. He plans to remain an agent there and continue to work his way up, networking all the way.

Indeed it is not difficult to picture Gulino ten years from now, dressed to kill in Armani, with a big cigar, representing celebrities. Gulino sensed that he had natural interpersonal and sales skills. He also knew he was not a "behind-the-desk-all-day" kind of person. He is someone who is aware of what he likes and what he is good at—the key to success in any career.

Jack Ford: From Lawyer to TV Player

Alternative Legal Career: NBC News Chief Legal Correspondent and co-Anchor of *Today, Weekend Edition*

Year Graduated From Law School: 1975

Law School Attended: Fordham

Years Practicing Law: Approximately eighteen

Jack Ford sits in his office in NBC's Rockefeller Center, surrounded by his awards (both television and legal), books and tapes for *Today Show* segments, and framed pictures of his family. His is a life that most lawyers would envy—and many aspire to.

But, he cautions the many lawyers who write to him, the transition from lawyer to NBC anchor does not happen overnight. "Don't say to yourself 'I'm going to quit practicing law tomorrow and the next day I'm going to start sending resumes to networks saying I'd like to anchor one of your shows,'" he advised. "The meteoric rise doesn't happen as meteorically as people think it does."

Jack's own progression happened gradually. After graduating from Yale, he attended Fordham University School of Law. He appeared several times on the quiz show *Jeopardy* during law school in order to help pay his tuition. He started his legal career as an Assistant Prosecutor in the Monmouth County (N.J.) Prosecutor's Office. Later, he became an accomplished trial attorney in New Jersey, arguing the successful defense of New Jersey's first death penalty case in 1983.

It was during this time that an unplanned "lucky break," which launched Jack's television career. The death penalty case garnered a lot of media attention, and when it was over, Jack was asked to do a lot of television interviews. One of them was with CBS anchor Jim Jenson. After the interview, Jenson, impressed with Jack's on-air personality, asked him if he would be interested in an interview with the news director to become CBS's legal commentator. He got the job. "I literally stumbled into television," he said." I never had any plans to get into it."

He was on the air once or twice a week and continued to maintain his full-time law practice for many years. He viewed television at the time as an adjunct to his legal career, rather than a new field. "It helped me, quite candidly, with juries. You would be picking a jury and they'd raise their hand and say, 'I know Mr. Ford; I don't know him personally, but I saw him on television'."

His broadcast career flourished at the same time as his legal career. Jack received an Emmy award in 1989. He also started moderating Fred Friendly's highly regarded series on PBS and was asked by Steven Brill in 1991 to become an anchor on a brand new network, Court TV. Jack anchored Court TV on a part-time basis, and was approached by NBC soon thereafter to become their legal commentator, starting on the *Today Show*.

"At that point, I was juggling a number of things...I was starting to realize it might be too many balls in the air. It may be time to make a choice." He decided to go with NBC on a full-time basis and to give up his law practice.

His timing could not have been better. Within months of his arrival, the O.J. Simpson case came to trial. Jack was all of the sudden on the air everyday, reporting on the case from New York and California. It put him directly in the spotlight and, like many others involved in the case, boosted his celebrity status. Midway through the Simpson trial, NBC offered him a chance to anchor the *Today Show*, the "best job in television," according to Jack.

Between the *Today Show* and the Simpson trial he was working a seven-day week and gaining tons of exposure on the air. "My *mother* said she was getting sick of seeing me everyday." After the Simpson trial, Jack settled into a regular position with NBC, working on various shows, including anchoring the weekend *Today Show*, and working on stories for *Dateline*, *MSNBC*, the *Nightly News*, and other shows. He has now established himself as both a legal expert and a general news anchor watched by millions of viewers each week.

His advice to lawyers who want to get into television? Many lawyers' biggest mistake is to underestimate the amount of time Jack, and others like him, needed to achieve national prominence. He emphasizes that it's not likely that anyone would go from never having done any television to anchoring the *Today Show*, as some lawyers who write to Jack would like to believe.

"I always say to people, here is what you should do—find yourself a *starting niche*. With the intro- duction of cable television there are all sorts of channels around that have their own sort of local news or talk shows."

The second step, according to Jack, is to establish yourself as an expert in some area of the law. For Jack, it was criminal law. "And then, you have to really sell yourself to a cable network or a local station as somebody who could provide some expertise." Eventu- ally, you build up a body of work and are sometimes able to move up to big- ger networks.

"I [always] illustrate and tell people about my friend Katie Couric, because people think all of a sudden she just ap-

Jack Ford's Progression from Lawyer to Full- Time Anchor:

- Assistant Prosecutor in the Monmouth County, NJ, Prosecutor's Office
- Criminal trial attorney
- CBS part-time legal commentator
- Court TV part-time anchor
- PBS
- NBC Legal Correspondent
- *Today* Show Anchor

peared as a major star on the *Today Show*. In reality, Katie started ten years before she ever got on the *Today Show* answering phones in a little station in Washington, DC...And whenever she could, she would tape a little segment of herself and put it on a demo reel...and ultimately got her shot at the networks."

Other colleagues who are lawyers have made the transi- tion through networks like Court TV and CNN as legal com- mentators. "There are a lot of people who have done it, but the formula has always been the same. They establish them- selves *first* in the practice of law as being talented in some area; they then use that talent and expertise and recognition to get them on the air as commentators and analysts."

Like most of the lawyers profiled in this book, Jack is happy with his new career outside of law practice. Although Jack sometimes still misses trying cases, he does not miss his life as a lawyer. His lament about how the practice changed in the 1980s, is common among lawyers. "I think it was a profession, now it is a business—that's very unfortunate."

A big plus of his new career is that he is still involved in law and legal issues without having to deal with the daily grind of practicing. Television also fulfills his love as a trial attorney of being out in the spotlight. "Instead of being in the spotlight in the courtroom with twelve jurors, every time you're on the air you have five, six, seven million people watching." The same intense, focused zone of concentration Jack experienced and relished while interviewing witnesses at trial is replicated when he is doing live interviews on television.

Finally, as busy as is his days are now, they have a definite beginning, middle, and end, unlike his days as a litigator. "At some point my day is over—[and] when it's over, it's over. I'm home with my family and I'm not returning a million calls from clients and not juggling the next day's witness list. The boundaries are frenetic, but there are boundaries."

Jack's transition was in some respects a product of luck and good timing. The use of legal experts on television as commentators had started at about the same time that he was spotted by Jim Jenson. He had already done quite a bit of television by the time Court TV went on the air. The O.J. Simpson trial started shortly after he joined NBC on a full-time basis. It doesn't hurt that Jack also has the all-American good looks and natural comfort in the spotlight that television requires.

But, he also worked very hard for a very long time to get to where he is now. Jack essentially worked at two careers on an almost full-time basis for many years before choosing television. Like many lawyers who have moved into another career, his transition out of law was very gradual, but ultimately very successful.

JOHN HART: FROM LAWYER TO POLITICIAN

Alternative Legal Career: Deputy Assistant to the President, Deputy Director of Intergovernmental Affairs, the White House

Year Graduated from Law School: 1987

Law School Attended: Fordham

Years Practicing Law: Approximately Five

"You need to work very hard to get lucky," John Hart says, sitting in his old-fashioned, spacious office in the old executive office building, overlooking the White House lawn. John has followed this credo to achieve a high-level position in the Clinton White House. In his position, John primarily serves as liaison on federal and state policy to state and local officials.

In John's case, it has not been all that long a road to the White House. Like many lawyers, an interest in politics had always been in the back of his mind. Starting back in his college days at Catholic University in Washington, D.C., he wrote his senior thesis on intergovernmental affairs, exploring how a state lobbies Washington.

After graduating from Fordham University School of Law, John clerked for the Hon. James T. Turner of the U.S. Court of Federal Claims. "I loved public service. I loved working in the chambers but that job paid only about $30,000. And so I had loans to pay off," he said. So as the clerkship ended, he was in the position, like most law graduates, of needing to make more money. John went to work as an associate for a seventy-lawyer Washington firm.

Unlike many young lawyers, however, he made a very conscious decision not to get caught up in the "golden handcuffs" and maintained a frugal lifestyle. He continued to approximate the life he had had as a $30,000-a-year law clerk, bankrolled the rest, and accelerated his law school loans to pay them back more quickly.

This proved to be a crucial step for Hart. When an opportunity came along later, John was able to take it, because he was in a position, financially, to be able to take a risk. While John was still working at the firm, he also kept up with the Washington contacts he had made during his college years. He started to do some networking with classmates from Fordham and Catholic, and people he had met who worked on the Hill.

After two years at the firm, John had to make a choice. "...they make the decision whether to make you partner or not after your seventh year. Am I going to dedicate my next three to four years to this or not?" As part of his decision-making process he continued to do some outreach, talking to people who were involved in all aspects of politics.

In 1991, he used some vacation time to attend a career/life planning retreat at Centerpoint, in Seattle, WA. (See chapter 4 for more information). "Being there and being away made me realize that there's a kind of a process for thinking through these things. What I was finding was not random, which is I want to have a structure and career path that is consistent with who I am, what my values are, and why I went to law school."

For John, that meant a career that was in some way involved with public service. After his vacation, he started to look into presidential campaigns as a way to get involved. He started looking at different candidates and talking to a lot of people, developing contacts at different campaigns. One night he came home, flipped on the TV, and happened to hear a speech that Bill Clinton was making. The issues and concerns that Clinton was addressing clicked with John's own belief system, and he started to look seriously into Clinton's campaign.

At the time, Clinton was "the way underdog," according to John. "Who was Clinton? Nobody had even heard of him. Where's Arkansas? Couldn't even find it on a map." One of John's social contacts at the time was George Stephanopolous. He had been friends with him shortly after college, when George was a fellow at the Disarmament Council, and they had kept in touch over the years.

George called John one night and told him that he was going to Arkansas to work on the Clinton campaign. He then talked with Clinton's campaign manager, David Wilhelm, who invited him down to work on the campaign. But there was a catch, as there often is in political campaigns. There was no salary waiting for him. If things worked out, he would probably get hired. If they didn't, he would be out of a job.

"It was time to fish or cut bait," John recalled. The fact that he had saved up his money and paid back some loans made his decision much more doable. He decided to take the risk. "I was literally making the jump and people were [saying], 'well, what are you going to do down there?' I could have been taking sandwich orders for all I knew. I'd never done a campaign, how do I know?"

Campaigns are difficult in many ways, but they are a meritocracy, according to John. The more you work, the more opportunities exist for you to make a name for yourself. "I worked very, very, hard when I got down there...I was the first one in and the last one out..," he said. He caught on quickly.

John was hired by the campaign after three weeks and became the person in charge of getting Clinton on the ballot in different states and organizing the

Hart's Advice to Lawyers Interested in Politics is:

- See where the need is and be ready to fill it
- Get in there, do the job well, and be flexible about what you do
- Do not get trapped by the "golden handcuffs"—maintain a fairly frugal lifestyle, so that you will have a chance to take risks when the opportunity arises
- Nothing ventured = nothing gained. As Hart himself found out, and advises others, "The greater the risk, can mean the greater the rewards."

delegates. He achieved the position of National Director of Delegate Operations, culminating in the nomination of Bill Clinton at the Democratic National Convention in New York, where Hart managed the convention floor operations.

John had met Clinton several times during the primary. Since the ballots for each state had to be signed and notarized, Hart and the notary would meet Clinton's plane in Arkansas at one or two in the morning when he returned from campaigning. When he brought the first one to Clinton for the state of New Hampshire, he said to Clinton, "Too late now, you can't back out." Clinton replied, "I don't intend to."

There is sometimes a shaky period in campaign politics, when your candidate has won, and you are not sure what your job, if any, will be next. For Hart, the long-range planning skills he had utilized in the campaign were put to use on the transition team. He became a senior member of then President-elect Clinton's transition staff, serving as Special Assistant to then-Transition Director Warren Christopher, and to Thomas "Mack" McLarty, following McLarty's appointment as Chief of Staff.

In January 1993, when Clinton took office, Hart was appointed to his current position in the Office of Intergovernmental Affairs. In 1995, he was asked by Clinton to also serve as his liaison to the Catholic community. Hart has a great interest in religion as well and is considering a greater involvement in that arena after politics.

In the meantime, Hart is enjoying his stint in the White House. As Clinton starts his second term as President of the United States, Hart is very well positioned to do more of what he likes best, either in politics or elsewhere in the public sector.

Larry Richard: From Lawyer to Psychologist

Alternative Legal Career: Psychologist and President of Richard Consulting Group

Law School Attended: University Of Pennsylvania

Year Graduated: 1972

Years Practicing Law: Approximately Ten Years

"Maybe it will get better," Larry Richard said to himself, many times during law school. Richard's father is a lawyer, and he had always dreamed of having a practice like his Dad. But law school felt forced, and it was very hard work. Not like the mandatory psychology course that he aced with ease in college.

In fact, he ended up being a double major, psychology and political science. He loved all of the psychology courses, but the political science courses were not enjoyable to him. "It should have been a 'V-8 moment'," he said, in retrospect. But his childhood vision of what it would be like to be a lawyer kept him going forward on that path for many years before he would follow his instincts.

After attending the University of Pennsylvania Law School, Richard practiced for almost ten years, trying four different types of legal positions. His goal was to get training in litigation, and afterward join his father's Philadelphia-area law firm. His first position was with the Pennsylvania Attorney General's Office as a civil litigator. "I felt very anxious and tense because there were so many things to keep track of...I don't have the kind of mind where I can keep all those things in track, and be organized in advance for that," he said." I enjoyed the [public] speaking part, but I didn't like the time pressure."

Richard was later to learn, as a psychologist, why that was so. In the meantime, he continued to pursue his legal career. He sensed that he was a "people person" and would enjoy a position that had more "collaborative interaction," and got a job working for Legal Aid. "I really had a sense of camaraderie with my colleagues. That was really satisfying, but it was still the same kind of work I was doing. I was going to court, only this time, as is the nature of Legal Aid, because you get three or four new clients a day, and each client requires weeks of preparation."

After two years, he left Legal Aid, in part because of burnout. " I look back at that time, and I think if I had continued to live that life I would be dead," he said. With almost five years of legal training behind him, he decided to finally join his dad's firm. It turned out to be very different from his childhood vision of law practice.

The only part of the job he really liked was the interaction with clients and the feeling that he was helping them with their problems. Everything else—the document drafting, the court rules, the research—was "horrible." He liked and respected his dad and his colleagues but hated what he was doing. He realized at that time that his feelings about law practice were not going to change. "If I'm hating my life, and I'm in the best of all possible places to practice law, then it's obvious that the only conclusion is law isn't for me."

He eventually left the firm, moved to New York, and did a brief stint in the entertainment business. He then became a solo practitioner for a while in New York, representing people in the entertainment business. He had not yet hit upon the right combination that would define his career goals. He knew that he liked psychology and working with people, and that he did not like litigation.

One day in the elevator at work, he overheard two Jesuit priests talking about starting a career counseling business called Mainstream Access. Fascinated, he made an immediate pitch to them in the elevator. He offered to barter his legal services to them in exchange for learning about the career counseling business. They were thrilled with his offer.

As part of his training with him, they administered several career "tests" to Richard. He was especially impressed with one called the Myers Briggs Type Indicator, from which he learned that his "type" would probably hate all of the details and deadlines involved in litigation. "I thought, boy, doesn't this explain a lot," he said. Intrigued with the idea of using testing to help people, he began to brainstorm about how he could use it in the legal profession.

He decided to get a graduate degree in psychology, and use it in some way to work with lawyers. In 1982 he started a doctoral program in organizational psychology at Temple University. On the way to getting his degree, he started a private career counseling business for lawyers in New York called Lawgistics. He later started to work with law firms and other organizations as his primary focus rather than counseling individuals. In 1993, he finally completed his dissertation and became Dr. Lawrence Richard, a psychologist who works with legal organizations. It had been almost twenty years since he had first thought about combining law and psychology as an undergraduate.

Since becoming a psychologist Richard has honed his mission to include "systemic positive changes in the legal profession using behavioral science." His goal is to change the legal profession to a model that is "more collaborative and one that is more humane."

It is a very lofty goal, but one Richard finds extremely fulfilling. After years of searching for the right career, he "feels like somebody who has died and came back and is living on borrowed time...I love what I'm doing." He is an example of a realistic career changer—someone who found his true calling not magically or instantaneously, but through a long process of slowly getting closer and closer to his ideal job.

Richard is also an example to lawyers who wonder if life gets any better outside of the law. When he was working at his dad's law firm, he used to watch the clock slowly moving, and taking forever to get to 5:00 or 6:00 p.m. (the earliest possible time he could leave). "I was just watching that thing going around the clock thinking there's this small group of people who love what they're doing, and I always thought it would be me...and I feel such a sense of loss that I'm not now one of those people even though I'm here where I thought I'd be having that experience," he said.

He is having that "experience" that he longed for now, as a psychologist. Had he not taken the risk inherent in change, he might not have ever found it.

Lesley Friedman: From Lawyer to Law Temp President

Alternative Legal Career: President and Founder, Special Counsel, a temporary agency for attorneys

Year Graduated From Law School:1985

Law School Attended: New York University

Years Practicing Law: Approximately Two Years

Lesley Friedman always knew she wanted to have her own business one day and quit law. And she did have her own business, and recently sold it—to the tune of $21 million. As the President of Special Counsel, one of the first temporary agencies for attorneys, she rode the crest of what would become a tidal wave in the world of hiring—the use of temporary, or "contract," attorneys to do legal work for major law firms and corporations.

Special Counsel was started by Friedman in 1987 two years after she graduated from law school. A graduate of N.Y.U. Law School, Friedman "hated practicing law." Her first legal job was at the now defunct Reavis & McGrath, in New York. She next went to work for another New York firm, Gelberg & Abrahms. Changing firms did not help. "Although the work environment was very nice and had a lot of perks, the work itself was very boring," she said. When Gelberg & Abrahms, the firm that she worked for, dissolved, Friedman decided to leave law practice and start her own business.

Friedman started her agency out of her Upper West Side apartment, with a post office box address on Park Avenue, where she would pick up her mail. She took out a $70,000 mortgage on her apartment. She met with potential placements in restaurants and upscale health clubs, and wore her mother's mink coat to meet with potential clients at law firms. From the moment she started, she marketed Special Counsel as a very exclusive, classy business that would appeal to lawyers.

At the time, it was still a "buyers' market" for lawyers. Lawyers who wanted to temp came to see Leslie because they were tired of practicing or wanted more free time to pursue family or creative interests. Partners in law firms had never heard of hiring "temp" lawyers, and in fact the New York City Bar Association issued an ethics opinion questioning the use of temporary attorneys at all.

At the time, other industry professionals "thought she was nuts," according to Friedman. Certainly they did not view her as any sort of competitive threat. In fact, during her first six months in business, she lost $13,000. The City Bar opinion threatened to destroy her business premise. The legal community was very resistant to the idea of temporary attorneys.

But then the recession in the legal industry started. Law firms began laying off associates and looking for ways to save money. Friedman sent out charts to the law firms, showing how much money they could save by using temporary attorneys. With Friedman's influence, the American Bar Association wrote a different opinion which offset the negative City Bar opinion, endorsing the use of temporary attorneys. Around 1990, the business became very successful. Mudge Rose, a large firm in New York, was her first "big" client.

From the very beginning, Friedman concentrated on utilizing her marketing skills. Special Counsel had very expensive-looking, classic, marketing materials from its inception. Friedman, who herself graduated in the middle of her class in law school (and failed the bar the first time around), would only use attorneys who went to top-ten law schools or graduated in the top 5 percent of their class. The Special Counsel brochure reads, "When Fortune 100 corporations and blue-chip law firms need temporary attorneys, they turn to Special Counsel—the service whose standards are as exacting as theirs."

She would Federal Express everything to clients (before the days of fax machines), and sent her clients clocks from Tiffany's as gifts. She did everything she could to appear professional and to appeal to the traditional large, credentials-conscious law firm. Friedman applied a marketing concept that she had picked up while working as a paralegal at Skadden Arps—exceptional attention to client interactions.

"I spent money I did not really have...I wanted to provide great client services," she said. By the early 1990s, her efforts had paid off, big-time. Special Counsel grew to the point where she had to hire a manager to help with the day-to-day operations of the business. She hired experienced lawyers to work as recruiters instead of hiring professional recruiters. Friedman loved the marketing aspect of business but did not like the management and accounting details that mushroomed when the business grew. She decided to sell the business and began to look for a buyer.

The sale of the business itself took two years. In August 1995, Friedman sold the business to a company called Accustaff. The sale, based in part on Special Counsel's revenues at the time, was for approximately $21 million. Although it remains Special Counsel, the new business is a "full-service" legal agency for secretaries, paralegals, and lawyers, very different from the original agency. She is not closely involved with the business at this point.

Friedman has moved to Florida and has taken some time for herself. A self-proclaimed workaholic, she is "just starting to relax." She is planning to take at least a year off. There are now several major temporary agencies which specialize in exclusively placing attorneys, and business is booming. The hiring of temporary attorneys by law firms has become quite acceptable. The City Bar has also become more accepting, and recently issued an opinion proclaiming that temporary attorneys who form a close relationship with the firm may refer to themselves as "Of Counsel" to the firm.

How did Friedman succeed? "I am a driven, ambitious person," she said. "I never gave up." During the early years of Special Counsel, she was motivated in part by fear: "I didn't want to ever go back to working for another person! ... I wanted control more than security." She also has a natural flair for and love of marketing. "Getting people to do something weird, and different, especially lawyers, who are stubborn," was the fun part, according to Friedman.

During the nine years that she ran Special Counsel, Friedman, who was in her thirties at the time, sacrificed her social life for the business. She worked most of the time, first at building the business, then at controlling what had become a large operation. "It was highly stressful," she said. "I took it all very seriously." Now in her early forties, she is taking time to catch up.

Friedman's advice to entrepreneurial lawyers? "You have to go out and try it. It will eventually lead to something else, like networking to find a job," she said. "It's a journey. You have to allow yourself to start it." Admittedly, it can be very painful, at first, not to have a big institution taking care of you, Friedman recalled. But the tradeoffs—control, being excited about what you do, and in Friedman's case, a big payoff, can make it very worthwhile.

LAWYERS AS ENTREPRENEURS

Although not everyone builds up a business worth $21 million, many lawyers have become entrepreneurs. They have become heads of lawyer and other recruitment agencies, restaurants, nightclubs, and many other business ventures. According to *Forbes* magazine (11/4/96 issue, "Make Lox, Not Law"), some of the businesses that lawyers have recently started include: a San Francisco based gift and housewares store with revenues of $5 million, a "seventies" music television promotion/mail order business which has sold more than 700,000 CDs, and a smoked fish business based in Atlanta which grossed approximately $1.2 million in 1996.

RICHARD ROBERTS: FROM RAINMAKER
TO PUBLIC POLICY ADVOCATE

Alternative Legal Career: Vice President, Government and Community Relations, Mount Sinai Medical Center

Law School Attended: Yale

Year Graduated From Law School: 1989

Years Practicing Law: Three +

The atmosphere at Mount Sinai Medical Center where Roberts works is very different from the corporate offices of Davis Polk & Wardwell, where Roberts began his legal career. The hospital occupies a series of buildings on several blocks near 101st and Fifth Avenue, which borders Harlem and the Upper East Side of New York. The streets outside the hospital are noisy and somewhat frenetic—everyone in the area is obviously connected with the hospital in some way.

Inside Robert's department, the atmosphere is quieter, but far from plush. The Department of Government and Community Relations occupies a set of offices, which appear to have been used previously as doctor's offices—in fact there is a sink right in the middle of Robert's office. The sink is now covered with law books as are the bookshelves and the desk that adjoin them. Many of the books deal with education law as well as health care.

Robert's job as Vice President of Government Relations and Community Affairs involves bringing together all of the various constituencies that are affected by the hospital and government reforms and legislation: the outlying community, the doctors, and hospital executives. As vice president, Roberts interacts with many different types of people. That is what Roberts has always liked to do, and has done successfully throughout his career.

"My theme has always been to try to keep in touch and develop contacts outside the 'box'—it always has led to something else," he said. Roberts has been involved in community activities since his first days as a lawyer when he started as an associate in the corporate department of Davis, Polk & Wardwell.

Although he had a very positive experience at DP&W, there were two down sides for Roberts: 1) the underlying subject matter, corporate law, was not intrinsically as interesting to Roberts as public policy; and 2) there was always a tension between the need to spend all of his time at the firm and his desire to pursue interests outside of the firm and with other people. For example, he was a member of the board of the Brooklyn Children's Museum at the time, something for which he had a strong interest.

One evening, he left the firm early for a board meeting, with the intention of returning to work afterward. It turned out a project came in for him while he was away that night. When he returned to the firm, it was clear that his colleagues were not pleased that he'd been away. Although he liked the firm, and they liked him as well, he decided to leave. Roberts wrote to Benno Schmidt, whom he had first met as an undergraduate residence counselor and then as a student leader of BLSA (Black Law Students Association) when Schmidt was Yale's President. Schmidt offered Roberts a job at the Edison Project (a start-up educational management company), working in the area of education policy.

"It was very difficult to leave [the firm]," he said. " I was actually shaking when I left... I was going into the great unknown, leaving a protected environment. However, the decision to do it once has made it easier to do it time and time again," he said.

Both of Robert's parents are teachers, and education policy was an area in which he had always been very interested. He was specifically interested in working with public policy involving communities and neighborhoods. The job fit in very closely with his beliefs, ideology, and interests. It was a very good career match. "There is nothing more neighborhood-based than a school," said Roberts.

After working with the Edison Project for about two years, one of the consultants to the project passed his resume on to New York city Mayor Guliani's administration. He was hired by the mayor, primarily to increase home ownership and revitalization in distressed neighborhoods throughout New York City. "Working in government with people setting public policy was what I really wanted to do...it was fantastic. One of the best work experiences I have ever had," he recalled. "I was the man from City Hall."

One of the people Roberts met through working for the mayor was on the Board of Mount Sinai. Again, networking led to his current position. He is thirty-two years old. He is now specializing in public policy as it relates to health care in a job that involves a lot of events, meetings, lunches, dinners, and political fundraisers. It also requires an in-depth knowledge of health care law and policy, which he continues to study.

The government relations part of his position involves co-ordinating the interaction with elected officials and the government regarding health care policy, legislation and regulatory matters. The community relations end of the job involves coordinating community outreach projects, mentoring programs, school based clinics and senior centers. There are approximately twelve people who now report to him.

In the future, Roberts may move into the senior management of Mount Sinai. Another possibility would be to move into a more senior-level position in external relations. "I'll be here for the foreseeable future," he said. He is in a position much coveted by other lawyers, as evidenced by the file he keeps with all of the resumes and letters that people have sent him wanting career advice. He actively maintains the file and tries to hook people up as often as he can.

Robert's advice to lawyers on how to develop contacts: Don't forget the people you knew before practicing law—keep up with them. "It's important to know as many people as possible," he said. Also, make time to get out of the firm—the most tempting thing is "to have breakfast, lunch and dinner at the firm," which is not conducive to making any outside connections.

Roberts has already in fact become a true external relations expert; his personal computerized Rolodex now contains 1,042 names. He keeps in touch with people he knows from college and law school on a regular basis and also still plays on the Davis Polk & Wardwell basketball team.

At the end of our interview, Roberts is off to yet another political event. At 8:00 p.m., his day is far from over. As we walk down Park Avenue, he points to a building that is involved in a controversy with the hospital. Despite the late hour, his enthusiasm for his job and his role in balancing the needs of the hospital and those of the surrounding community is apparent.

MINDY BASS: FROM LAWYER TO PROGRAM COORIDNATOR

Alternative Legal Career: Program Coordinator, Lawyers in Transition [LIT] Committee, Association of the Bar of the City of New York

Year Graduated From Law School: 1993

Years Practicing Law: Two

Mindy Bass knew from the very start that she might not practice law. Like many recent college graduates, she thought a law degree would give her the credibility to pursue a variety of options. A psychology major at SUNY Binghamton, Bass always liked working with people. She thought law school would be an interesting path to furthering her career objectives, and entered Cardozo Law School in 1990.

After spending law school summers clerking for a judge and working for a small medical malpractice firm, Bass took a job with a personal injury firm after graduation. "I took the first thing that jumped at me," she said. "It was a big mistake." She left after about a year. "If I had really loved it, it would have looked good on my resume [to stay]." But her heart was not in it.

Like many law students, Bass was not focused on her own likes and dislikes, but on what the job market offered. However, her unhappiness propelled her to think about what she wanted to do. She networked with people in her law school career planning center, read *The New York Times* Sunday classified ads from cover to cover, just looking for ideas. She decided she wanted to find a job where she could work with people.

After a brief stint with a legal placement agency she was back in the job hunt again. "It turned out to be all sales," she said. Her turning point came when she interviewed with a law firm and, at the end, sensing her ambivalence, the interviewer told her, "You don't really want to work here." The interviewer then spent some time brainstorming with Bass, suggesting she do pro bono work and take continuing legal education courses.

"Everything that had happened to me pushed me further and further away from the law," Bass said. Ironically, what she really did not like about practicing law turned out to be the very thing she loves about the job she now holds at the Bar Association. According to Bass, she is making the equivalent of what she would make at a small law firm and the transition from lawyer to bar association executive wasn't very difficult. She had several transferable skills, including knowledge of the legal profession and the Bar Association structure, as well as the ability to relate to lawyers. She also was adept at program planning and had volunteered at the organization prior to her interview.

Working at a Bar Association

What could you do at the Bar Association? Below are some possible jobs you may want to look in to:
- Director, Programming
- Director, Continuing Legal Education
- Director, Bar Fund (fund-raising)
- Director, Community Outreach Programs
- Communications Director
- Meeting Services Director
- Staff Attorney
- Executive Director

Carol Kanarek: From Lawyer to Legal Career Counselor

Alternative Legal Career: Legal Career Counselor

Year Graduated from Law School: 1979

Law School Attended: University of Michigan

Years Practicing Law: Approximately two-and-a-half years

Carol Kanarek is kind of the Faith Popcorn of the world of lawyers, predicting trends in the legal market for her clients. Her agency provides outplacement services to lawyers who are asked to leave their firms, either because the firm is downsizing, or the relationship did not turn out to be a good match. Outplacement is usually provided to lawyers leaving large law firms or corporations as part of their severance package. It involves meeting with an outplacement agency, in this case Kanarek's, on an ongoing basis for career counseling and other job related services.

Kanarek started her business in 1984 with a partner Jude Shaw whom she met at a previous job in legal publishing. They decided to start a legal recruitment business for attorneys and law firm administrators. Kanarek had previously worked as a corporate associate at Thacher Profit & Wood in New York and as Director of Career Services at New York Law School. Her partner, Shaw, had been a recruiting coordinator at a law firm. They hit it off right from the start. "We really clicked, and we saw right away that we would be complementary to each other...," she said. They started the business by keeping expenses and overhead very low with very simple offices and no support staff. They also started the business when they had already been working in their careers for long enough to establish a good track record. They knew that they could probably return to their respective careers if the business did not work out.

Their concept was unique. "Initially our idea was that we were going to be a placement firm and not a headhunting firm...and that we were going to provide extra special customized service to the people we worked with." They told potential clients (law firms) that anyone that was sent to them was well worth interviewing, and that they would guarantee not to waste their time. On the candidate's side, they focused on giving them a broad view of the market as a whole.

"I think that one of the ways in which we were successful was by having the attitude that, sure, we'd like to place you, but the most important thing is that you find the right job," she said. Even if they did not make a placement, they reasoned, they would make a good impression. People would remember them and give them referrals. The concept worked.

Kanarek & Shaw became a hit. They continued to work at building the firm, concentrating on exceptional client services. Their marketing strategy, ironically, was not to market themselves too aggressively. They maintained their soft-sell approach. It worked, somewhat to Kanarek's own surprise. "I was one of those people that...when I was a Brownie, I was not able to sell my quota of cookies so my mother would have a freezer full of thin mints because I was such a non-sales person. So my orientation always towards the business was, you distinguish yourself in a positive way by the service you provide."

Kanarek's background as a lawyer at a prestigious firm, also helped business. "It is helpful both from an employer and an individual lawyer perspective that you can, when you're around them (lawyers), walk the walk and talk the talk. And that makes a big difference, and it puts people at ease...because you've been there," she said.

In the mid 1980s, the focus of Kanarek's business changed. Although both she and her partner continued to make attorney and law firm administrator placements, the firms began to lay off many of the excess attorneys they had hired when business was better. Law firms began to approach them to do outplacement instead of placements at the firm. Kanarek's counseling background and her knowledge of the legal job market proved a good combination for the field of outplacement.

But the turn the business took was somewhat of a surprise to her, as lawyer layoffs were to the entire legal community when they began. "What I do now didn't even exist when I was in law school. The whole concept of outplacement is really a child of the boom years of the eighties when the firms started to heavily leverage themselves and the one-to-one associate-partner ratio went out the window. And when they started to realize they created a monster that they felt very guilty about, that was when a couple of firms came to me initially," she said.

For a while, Kanarek and Shaw continued to do both recruitment and outplacement, but when Shaw left the business for personal reasons, and the need for outplacement grew, Kanarek focused exclusively on outplacement and consulting work. Her now solo outplacement business has continued to be very successful and has maintained the professional image that it started with.

Although Kanarek did not especially like law practice, and does not miss her days as a corporate associate, she has no regrets about having practiced law for several years before leaving. "I wanted to stay long enough to really feel like I had mastered things and that I was successful at doing it, even though I didn't like it," she said. "It was very important for me to get to the point that when I did leave, they would be sorry to see me go...I still have many good friends at the firm." The firm also remains one of her major clients to this day.

Kanarek, always an expert on legal market trends, is now using that knowledge to help lawyers identify potential positions. "A lot of my focus now is on longitudinal things, which is helping people to identify rapidly developing companies that may not have in-house [counsel], rather than just the traditional, let's see where there's a job...helping people to analyze the marketplace." Next, people have to figure out how to market themselves to the employer, according to Kanarek, not as a "sales job," but a way to present themselves as someone who can fill a need, solve problems, and do the job faster and cheaper. Her advice to lawyers is similar to the route she herself took in starting her business and adjusting it to changing market trends.

Kanarek's Advice to Lawyers Wishing to Leave Law Practice:

- Don't let yourself become too immersed in the lawyer "lifestyle", or it will be harder for you to leave. Try to living within, or below your means.
- Learn to identify what it is that you are trying to emulate so that you can functionalize your background to make sense in the new world that you are trying to enter. You have to learn to walk and talk like the people in that different world.

Kanarek, who is known for her kindness as much as she is for her superior knowledge of the job market, remains a soft touch, sensitive to the needs of lawyers. "Because every time I see somebody who is junior and has been fired, I think, and I've seen hundreds of them now...I never fail to have this sort of little pang of, what if that had happened to me. And I try to make people realize that this is a systemic thing, and it is not their fault."

Sample Resumes

7

Basic Resume Template for an Attorney

Name _____

Address
Home Phone
Business Phone

BAR STATUS

> List Bar(s) you have been admitted to.

(or)

LEGAL EXPERIENCE

> **Employer Name**   City, St
> Your title   Dates
> • Using bullets, describe your experience. Remember, use action verbs!
> •
> •

> **Employer Name**   City, St
> Your Title   Dates
> •
> •
> •

ADDITIONAL EXPERIENCE

> **Employer Name**   City, St   Dates
> Your Title
> •
> •
> •

EDUCATION

> **School Name**
> List Law school and degree received
> **Class Standing:**
> Top percentage listing acceptable
> **Honors:**
> List any honors you've received here (i.e., Dean's List, etc.)
> **Activities:**
> List any organizations, associations, or projects you've worked with here (i.e., Editor, *Urban Law Journal*; Black Student Associations, etc.)

> **School Name**
> List undergraduate institution
> **Major:**   **Minor:**

> **Honors:**
> (List here)
> **Activities:**
> (List here)

PERSONAL

> List any personal interests here (i.e., English literature, golf, volunteer work, etc.)

TRANSITION FROM LAW TO BUSINESS

BOB SMITH

5 Willow Drive
Chelmsford, MA 01763

Home: (617) 232-2222
Office: (617) 546-4444

INDUSTRY KNOWLEDGE/LEGAL EXPERIENCE

- Extensive knowledge of the insurance industry and coverage issues involving general liability insurance policies.
- Strong knowledge of products liability insurance law.
- Comprehensive knowledge or environmental regulations including CERCLA (Superfund) and RCRA.
- Experience in handling all aspects of complex litigation, including setting strategies and managing cases autonomously, developing project budgets, researching and drafting legal memoranda and briefs.

DEMONSTRATED BUSINESS SKILLS

- Communicating effectively and persuasively: Drafted memoranda, briefs, pleadings and correspondence. Crafted two-volume affidavit highlighting inconsistent positions used by insurance companies in environmental insurance coverage cases which became the model used firm-wide.
- Developing project strategies and supervising staff: Managed 14 employees while conducting multi-million dollar Document production for environmental insurance litigation. Designed and implemented document management plan that saved client $40,000 in shipping costs alone.
- Preparing cost-benefit analyses: Analyzed data, identified available legal alternatives and drafted opinion letter for Fortune 500 client addressing environmental issues under CERCLA (Superfund). Determined the most effective course of action saving client approximately $750,000 in legal costs.
- Interviewing techniques: Determined pertinent information to be obtained from clients and hostile witnesses, prepared questions and conducted depositions relating to environmental insurance coverage actions.
- Negotiating agreements: Negotiated and researched agreements with opposing parties' counsel regarding disputed legal issues.
- Researching: Proficient at conducting research using online computer databases (Nexis/Lexis and Westlaw) and traditional sources (books, periodicals and document repositories). Searched legal and non-legal resources, analyzed materials and applied relevant findings to legal issues relating to all aspects of complex litigation.

WORK HISTORY

Charles, James & Johnson, P.C., Associate, October 1992 to Present, Summer Associate, 1991
Oversee all phases of complex litigation.

Other Law Related Employment
Mayor John Samuels Interim Transition Team, Fall 1994, Consultant
American Bar Association, Summer 1991, Political Asylum Pro Bono Volunteer
New York Bar Association, Spring 1991, Tenant Litigation Pro Bono Volunteer
Fordham Law Professor Michelle Goldsmith, Summer 1990, English Legal History Research Assistant
Blue and White, Attorneys at Law, August 1988 to May 1989, Immigration Law Legal Assistant

Financed undergraduate and graduate degrees through various summer employment positions.

EDUCATION

FORDHAM UNIVERSITY SCHOOL OF LAW, New York, NY
Juris Doctor - May 1992; Admitted to New York and New Jersey Bars
Activities: Environmental Law Report, Member
            Litigation Skills and Mediation Clinics, Student Attorney

THE GEORGE WASHINGTON UNIVERSITY, Washington, D.C.
Bachelor of Business Administration - May 1989, Cum Laude, Inetrnational Business - Finance

TRANSITION FROM LAW TO PRIVATE BANKING

Mary Banks
22 Spring Lane Road
Goshen, New York 10562
Home: (914) 999-0000
Office: (212) 222-8888

SUMMARY OF QUALIFICATIONS

- Manage relationships with private banking trust and estate clients

- Write clear and persuasive reports and correspondence

- Coordinate account administration with attorneys, outside experts and banking professionals

PROFESSIONAL EXPERIENCE

MORGAN GUARANTY TRUST COMPANY OF NEW YORK
1989 to present
Client Manager

Responsible for the management of 200 trust, estate and charitable accounts with average value of $7,000,000. Work directly with clients, attorneys and co-trustees as well as investment and tax experts. Coordinate valuing of estate assets with real estate and art appraisers. Train administrative and support staff.

- Member of 3 person team handling new family relationship worth $200,000,000. Administer estate and resulting trusts benefitting family members, charities and scientific research facility. Meet with clients periodically to review their investments and estate plans. Developed specialized account reports based on feedback elicited from family.

- Analyzed financial circumstances of several clients requesting trust withdrawals; helped them create plans for reducing debt. Wrote reports advocating appropriate withdrawals which were approved by trust supervisory committee.

- Met with trust beneficiary confined to psychiatric institution and his psychologists and social workers to evaluate his needs firsthand. Coordinated budget and living arrangements to take effect on his release, and made successful presentation of plan to trust supervisory committee.

LOPPMAN & PAWLINGS
1986 to 1989
Associate

As trusts and estates attorney in New York law firm drafted wills and trust instruments. Handled all aspects of estate administration including court probate proceedings, preparation of estate tax returns and negotiations with IRS. Researched various legal issues and wrote internal memoranda and briefs submitted to court.

EDUCATION

Brown University   J.D. 1986

University of Pennsylvania B.A. in History, 1982

TRANSITION FROM LAW TO PUBLIC RELATIONS

Maria Gonzalez

66 Ocean Avenue   (H) 203/555-5555
Hillside, New York 10538   (O) 914/555-1234

Results-oriented attorney with extensive public relations experience who works well
with people to achieve goals.

ACCOMPLISHED HIGHLIGHTS

Marketing/Public Relations

- Press conferences and special events staged worldwide
- Comprehensive customer relations program initiated
- Editorial material researched, created, and placed on a global basis

Counseling

- Advised a broad spectrum of clients
- Gained confidence of children and young adults as their advocate
- Enriched students' learning experience
- Served as parents' diagnostic adviser
- Acted as liaison between entry-level law clerks and chief judge

Writing/Public Speaking

- Drafted civil, juvenile, and matrimonial memoranda, motions, orders, and decisions
- Prepared offering circular, and supporting documents
- Prepared and delivered presentations to diverse audiences throughout the world

EMPLOYMENT

Solo Practitioner	1992–Present	Law Guardian
Whitman & White	1991	Associate
New York Supreme Court	1990	Law Secretary
Maine Circuit Court	1988–1990	Chief Law Clerk
Jones and Reese	1987–1988	Associate
OMB	1976–1986	Senior Publicist
St. Thomas Law School	1974–1976	Educator

EDUCATION

Syracuse University School of Law, J.D.
University of Minnesota, B.S

PAUL M. HASTINGS

80 Central Park West
New York, NY 10023

Tel. (212) 555-1212
E-mail: pmh1@aol.com

PROFILE:

Employment and litigation attorney with human resources and recruiting/placement industry experience; combines excellent oral and written communication skills with ability to inspire client and colleague confidence.

MARKETING AND HUMAN RESOURCES EXPERIENCE:

ATTORNEYTEMP, INC., Contract and Permanent Legal Placement, New York, NY

Director of Marketing   April 1995-May 1996

Marketed contract/temporary attorney and paralegal concept to law firms and corporate law departments through sales presentations and targeted mailings, attendance at and participation in attorney-attended functions, personal networking and extensive cold-calling and follow-up. Established and nurtured relationships with key decision-makers at law firms and corporations within New York City and Westchester and Fairfield County markets.

OSBORNE, HILL & OWENS, Public Relations, New York, NY

Director of Human Resources   October 1993-June 1994

Responsible for all human resource and benefit functions for 200-person firm with five offices in the United States. Interpreted employee policies and benefit developments and issued written communications regarding same. Standardized medical leave policy in cases of pregnancy-related disabilities, which clarified policy and reduced potential for liability. Promulgated extensive revisions to employee handbook. Negotiated employment contracts. Initiated diversity hiring and recruitment program, achieving goal in New York within six weeks.

LEGAL EXPERIENCE:

ATTORNEY (self employed)   July 1994-present

· *Of Counsel*, **O'KEEFE & MILBOURNE**, employment litigation attorneys (management side). 5/96-present

· *Consultant*, **CORPCO** (drafted employment law compliance program). 11/94-2/95

· Service private clients; render legal services pro bono for various non-profit organizations. 7/94-present

SULLIVAN & O'CONNOR, New York, NY

Associate Attorney (Employment Law/ Litigation   September 1989-October 1993

Represented employers in employment discrimination and other commercial litigation and advised clients on issues involving federal, state and local fair employment laws. Counseled employers on pre-termination decisions and conducted investigations into post-termination charges of discrimination. Wrote employee policies and documents relating to hiring and termination. Appeared in various courts and had supervisory responsibility for all phases of pre-trial discovery. Second-chaired two federal jury trials. Managed paralegals and junior associates.

FRIEDMAN & GOLD, New York, NY

Associate Attorney (Litigation)   September 1987-August 1989

Research, writing, document review and trial preparation in employment discrimination and other litigation.

EDUCATION:

NEW YORK UNIVERSITY SCHOOL OF LAW, J.D., 1987

· Articles Editor, *Fordham International Law Journal*

· Teaching Assistant, First-Year Legal Writing

TRINITY COLLEGE, A.B., American Studies, 1984

BEFORE: TRANSITION FROM ENTERTAINMENT
LAWYER TO AGENT

Roger A. Smith
145 West 83rd Street, Apt. 24
New York, New York 10023
212.555.5555

ENTERTAINMENT EXPERIENCE

I have represented a number of entertainers and have assisted them in both their legal and business affairs. In particular, I have been responsible for negotiating and drafting deal memoranda, finance agreements, option agreements, music publishing agreements, recording contracts, management contracts, merchandise agreements, partnership agreements and employment contracts. Legal entities I handled involved such entities as New Kids on the Block, Pat Benatar, Roomful of Blues, Rounder Records, Blacktop Records, Fantasy Records, Planet Dallas Music Publishing, Rock 'N Roll USA, and Hemdale Films. As a result of my work, I have received legal credits on videos and commercially distributed recordings.

EMPLOYMENT

William Morris Agency, Inc., New York, NY
    Agent, Licensing and Merchandising Department   1996–Present
    Agent Training Program, Agent Trainee   1996–1996

Fifi Oscard Agency, Inc., New York, NY   1993
    Legal Counsel & Assistant Agent to Fifi Oscard

LeBoeuf, Lamb, Leiby & MacRae, New York, NY   1991–1992
    Associate Attorney, General Corporate Finance Practice

Mudge Rose Guthrie Alexander & Ferdon, New York, NY   1989–1991
    Associate Attorney, General Corporate Finance Practice

Lewin & Rosenthal, Boston, MA   1988
    Extern Entertainment Law Practice

EDUCATION

Boston College Law School, Juris Doctor, May 1989, Newton Center, MA
    Uniform Commercial Code Reporter-Digest, Associate Editor, Staff Writer
    Arts, Entertainment & Sports Law Society, Founder & Chairman

Boston College, Bachelor of Arts, Magna cum laude, May 1986, Chestnut Hill, MA
    Dual Degrees: Economics & Philosophy
    Student Government Vice President of Programming

CREDENTIALS

Admitted to Practice: New York, Massachusetts

Writers Guild of America. Literary Agent/Signatory

American Bar Association: Forum Committee, Entertainment & Sports Law

New York State Bar Association: Entertainment & Sports Law Section

Volunteer Lawyers for the Arts

After: Transition from Entertainment Lawyer to Agent

Roger A. Smith
145 West 83rd Street, Apt. 24
New York, New York 10023
(212) 555-5555

EMPLOYMENT

Fifi Oscard Agency, Inc., Assistant to Fifi Oscard/Junior Agent, New York, NY

LeBoeuf, Lamb, Leiby & MacRae, Attorney, New York, NY

Mudge Rose Guthrie Alexander & Ferdon, Attorney, New York, NY

Lewin & Rosenthal, Law Clerk, Boston, MA

EXPERIENCE

- Represented motion picture, television and literary properties and rights
- Motion Picture, television, theatrical, voice-over and commercial submissions
- Scouting and talent development in the areas of film, television and music
- Negotiate, review and draft agency agreements
- Review SAG, AFTRA and AEA contracts
- Research and draft literary and motion picture rights option agreements
- Negotiate and review draft book publishing contracts
- Negotiate and review draft producer, director and writer contracts
- Negotiate and review draft film financing agreements
- Negotiate and review draft recording contracts
- Negotiate and review draft music publishing agreements
- Negotiate and review draft management agreements
- Review and draft limited partnership agreements
- Negotiate and review draft merchandise contractst
- Review and draft partnership agreements
- Draft minor's contract court petitions
- Negotiate and review draft and draft various deal memoranda
- Prepare and draft script treatments

EDUCATION

Boston College Law School, Newton Center, MA
J.D., May 1989
- Booked lecturers and entertainers for academic and social functions

Boston College, Chestnut Hill, MA
B.A., Economics, Philosophy, *magna cum laude*, May 1986
- Organized and booked social, academic and cultural programs
- Booked band "Manoverboard"

BEFORE: TRANSITION FROM LAW TO PUBLISHING

JOAN SMITH
888 East 72nd Street
New York, New York 10021
(212) 555-5555

LEGAL EXPERIENCE

BIGGS & LITTLER, New York, New York
Associate: August 1993 to present

LINCOLN, BLINKEN & NODD, New York, New York
Associate: January 1990 to July 1993

FRANK & STEIN, New York, New York
Associate: September 1987 to July 1988

Areas of Expertise: Litigation of corporate, securities, antitrust, bankruptcy, copyright, trademark, labor and employment, and civil rights matters; administrative proceeding

• Examined witnesses at trials and hearings. Conducted research and drafted pretrial and post-trial briefs. Prepared stipulations of fact.

• Negotiated settlements. Drafted settlement papers.

• Drafted affidavits and memoranda of law, conducted research, and argued motions for temporary restraining orders, preliminary injunctions, summary judgment, and change of venue, and motions related to discovery matters.

• Conducted and defended depositions. Negotiated the scope of discovery requests. Drafted interrogatories, answers to interrogatories, requests for documents, and deposition notices. Reviewed documents in connection with discovery requests.

• Drafted complaints and answers.

LEGAL PUBLISHING CO., INC., New York, New York
Legal Editor: August 1988 to December 1989

• Wrote and edited sections of treatises on the Federal Rules of Civil Procedure and on practice before the National Labor Relations Board.

OTHER EXPERIENCE

NEW YORK CITY HIGH SCHOOL, Brooklyn, New York
Teacher and Union Representative: September 1980 to June 1984

• Created writing exercises and evaluated students' writing ability. Advised students regarding their career goals and choice of university; prepared a workbook to guide their decision-making.

• Negotiated salary and benefits issues in connection with contract renewal. Developed union policy with respect to promotion. Created and wrote a monthly newsletter regarding recent union activities and their effect on members' rights. Participated in union meetings.

EDUCATION

NEW YORK STATE LAW SCHOOL, New York, New York
J.D., 1987

Honors: *New York State Law Review*, Articles Editor

Publications: "Note, Pendent Jurisdiction -- The Wave of the Future in Bringing Parties into Federal Court," 323 *New York State Law Review* 229 (1986)

Activities: Moot Court

CALIFORNIA COLLEGE, Los Angeles, California
B.A., *cum laude*, in English Literature 1980

Honors: Phi Beta Kappa

(Joan Smith resumes courtesy of Linda E. Laufer, career counselor & V.P., Partners In Law Placement, Inc.)

During (Stage 1): Transition from Law to Publishing

JOAN SMITH
888 East 72nd Street
New York, New York 10021
(212) 555-5555

LEGAL EXPERIENCE
Areas of expertise: Litigation of corporate, securities, antitrust, bankruptcy, copyright, trademark, labor and employment, and civil rights matters; administrative proceedings.

- Examined witnesses at trials and hearings. Conducted research and drafted pretrial and post-trial briefs. Prepared stipulations of fact.

- Negotiated settlements. Drafted settlement papers.

- Drafted affidavits and memoranda of law, conducted research, and argued motions for temporary restraining orders, preliminary injunctions, summary judgment, and change of venue, and motions related to discovery matters.

- Conducted and defended depositions. Negotiated the scope of discovery requests. Drafted interrogatories, answers to interrogatories, requests for documents, and deposition notices. Reviewed documents in connection with discovery requests.

- Drafted complaints and answers.

- Wrote and edited sections of treatises on the Federal Rules of Civil Procedure and on practice before the National Labor Relations Board.

OTHER EXPERIENCE
Taught English to high school students and served as a teachers' union representative.

- Created writing exercises and evaluated students' writing ability. Advised students regarding their career goals and choice of university; prepared a workbook to guide their decision-making.

- Negotiated salary and benefits issues in connection with contract renewal. Developed union policy with respect to promotion. Created and wrote a monthly newsletter regarding recent union activities and their effect on members' rights. Participated in union meetings.

EMPLOYMENT HISTORY
Attorney: **Biggs & Littler**, New York, New York, August 1993 to present; **Lincoln, Blinken & Nodd**, New York, New York, January 1990 to July 1993; **Frank & Stein**, New York, New York, September 1987 to July 1988

Legal Editor: **Legal Publishing Co., Inc.**, New York, NY, August 1988 to December 1989

Teacher: **New York City High School**, Brooklyn, NY, September 1980 to June 1984

EDUCATION
NEW YORK STATE LAW SCHOOL, New York, New York
J.D., 1987
Honors: *New York State Law Review*, Articles Editor
Publications: "Note, Pendent Jurisdiction -- The Wave of the Future in Bringing Parties into Federal Court, 323 *New York State Law Review* 229 (1986)
Activities: Moot Court

CALIFORNIA COLLEGE, Los Angeles, California
B.A., *cum laude*, in English Literature 1980
Honors: Phi Beta Kappa

DURING (STAGE 2): TRANSITION FROM LAW TO PUBLISHING

JOAN SMITH
888 East 72nd Street
New York, New York 10021
(212) 555-5555

WRITING AND EDITING EXPERIENCE

Wrote and edited newspaper articles and professional materials.

- Wrote articles on local political issues for a widely circulated weekly newspaper in Manhattan. Created and wrote a monthly newsletter regarding recent union activities and their effect on members' rights. Prepared and edited articles and columns for a newspaper published three times a week during all four years of college.

- Prepared 11 articles for a column in the New York Law Journal.

- Wrote and edited sections of legal treatises related to procedures to be followed in the federal courts and before an administrative agency. Reviewed, revised, reorganized and incorporated text written by free lance authors. Resolved substantive and editorial issues through ongoing consultations with authors.

LEGAL AND OTHER EXPERIENCE

Litigated copyright, trademark, civil rights, corporate, and labor and employment matters. Taught English to high school students and served as a teachers' union representative.

- Drafted pretrial and post-trial briefs, stipulations of fact, settlement papers, affidavits and memoranda of law with respect to motions, discovery documents and pleadings. Conducted research. Examined witnesses at trials and hearings. Negotiated settlements. Argued motions. Conducted and defended depositions. Negotiated the scope of discovery requests.

- Created writing exercises and evaluated students' writing ability. Advised students regarding their career goals and choice of university; prepared a workbook to guide their decision-making. Negotiated salary and benefits issues in connection with contract renewal. Developed union policy with respect to promotion. Participated in union meetings.

EMPLOYMENT HISTORY

Writer/Editor: **Manhattan Weekly Newspaper**, New York, New York, September 1990 to present [Staff Writer]; **Legal Publishing Co.**, Inc., New York, New York, August 1988 to December 1989 [Legal Editor]

Attorney: **Biggs & Littler**, New York, New York, August 1993 to present; **Lincoln, Blinken & Nodd**, New York, New York, January 1990 to July 1993; **Frank & Stein**, New York, New York, September 1987 to July 1988

Teacher: **New York City High School**, Brooklyn, New York, September 1980 to June 1984

EDUCATION

NEW YORK STATE LAW SCHOOL, New York, New York
J.D., 1987
Honors: *New York State Law Review*, Articles Editor
Publications: "Note, Pendent Jurisdiction -- The Wave of the Future in Bringing Parties into Federal Court," 323 *New York State Law Review* 229 (1986)
Activities: Moot Court

CALIFORNIA COLLEGE, Los Angeles, California
B.A., *cum laude*, in English Literature 1980
Honors: Phi Beta Kappa

After: Transition from Law to Publishing

JOAN SMITH
888 East 72nd Street
New York, New York 10021
(212) 555-5555

PUBLISHING EXPERIENCE

NATIONAL WEEKLY MAGAZINE, New York, New York
Features Writer: June 1996 to present
Wrote articles regarding national politics including the 1996 Presidential campaign debates, the strategies pursued by Congressional leaders with respect to balancing the budget and tax reform, and the effect of lobbyists on current gun control legislation. Interviewed members of Congress and other national political figures.

MANHATTAN WEEKLY NEWSPAPER, New York, New York
Staff Writer: September 1990 to May 1996
Wrote articles on local political issues, including proposed ways to reduce crimes, cuts in spending on education, landlord-tenant disputes and compliance with zoning ordinances.

LEGAL PUBLISHING CO., INC., New York, New York
Legal Editor: August 1988 to December 1989
Wrote and edited sections of legal treatises on litigation procedural matters. Reviewed, revised, reorganized and incorporated text written by free lance authors. Resolved substantive and editorial issues through ongoing consultations with authors.

LEGAL AND OTHER EXPERIENCE

BIGGS & LITTLER, New York, New York
Litigation Associate, Corporate and Copyright and Trademark Law: August 1993 to May 1996

LINCOLN, BLINKEN & NODD, New York, New York
Corporate and Securities Litigation Associate: January 1990 to July 1993

FRANK & STEIN, New York, New York
Associate: September 1987 to July 1988

• Prepared 11 articles for publication in the New York Law Journal.

• Conducted research and drafted briefs, affidavits and memoranda of law, and other litigation documents. Examined witnesses at trials and hearings. Negotiated settlements. Argued motions. Conducted and defended depositions.

NEW YORK CITY HIGH SCHOOL, Brooklyn, New York
Teacher and Union Representative: September 1980 to June 1984
• Created writing exercises and evaluated students' writing ability. Advised students regarding career goals and choice of university; prepared a workbook to guide them.

• Created and wrote a monthly newsletter regarding recent union activities and their effect on members' rights. Negotiated salary and benefits issues in connection with contract renewal. Developed union policy with respect to promotion.

EDUCATION

NEW YORK STATE LAW SCHOOL, New York, New York
J.D., 1987
Honors: *New York State Law Review*, Articles Editor
Publications: "Note, Pendent Jurisdiction -- The Wave of the Future in Bringing Parties into Federal Court," 323 *New York State Law Review* 229 (1986)

CALIFORNIA COLLEGE, Los Angeles, California
B.A., **cum laude**, in English Literature 1980; Phi Beta Kappa; *The Quidnunc*, student newspaper, various editorial positions

Non-Practicing Famous Lawyers

(Note: some of the following people practiced law, others only had legal training or did not finish law school).

WRITERS/EDITORS

John Grisham, Author, *The Firm*, *The Rainmaker*, and many other bestsellers

Scott Turow[1], Author, *Presumed Innocent*, *Pleading Guilty*, and *The Laws of Our Fathers*

Steve Martini, Author, *Undue Influence**

John Kennedy, **Jr**, Editor, *George* magazine

---

[1]As a sidenote, John Grisham, Scott Turow, and Steve Martini are not alone. The number of lawyers publishing legal thrillers is burgeoning. In fact, there are enough in print to constitute a special section in the bookstore. Recent lawyer/legal thriller authors also include Robert Tanenbaum, *Falsely Accused* (formerly a Manhattan A.D.A. and mayor, Beverly Hills), Lisa Scottoline, *Legal Tender*, (formerly an associate at a law firm in Philadelphia), and Michael C. Eberhard, *Against the Law*. In addition, the post-O.J. era has produced writing opportunities for many prominent criminal lawyers, including Christopher Darden, Johnnie Cochran, and Gerry Spence.

Mortimer Zuckerman, owner, *U.S. News and World Report* (Was quoted as saying that he gave up his legal practice when he realized that it was the exact opposite of sex; "Even when it's good, it's lousy.")

Franz Kafka, writer (worked full-time as lawyer at an insurance company and wrote at night)

Jules Verne, writer

Henry James, writer

Wallace Stevens, poet

Also, **Moliere**, **Balzac**, **Robert Louis Stevenson**

MEDIA PERSONALITIES

Geraldo Rivera, talk show host/anchor, Court TV show host

Catherine Crier, anchor, Fox (formerly at ABC and CNN)

Jeff Greenfield, Political Commentator, ABC ("Nightline", etc.)

Jack Ford, Chief Legal Correspondent, "Today" show Co-Anchor, NBC

SPORTS:

Paul Tagliabue, NFL Commissioner

Tony LaRussa, Manager, St. Louis Cardinals

Howard Cosell, Sportscaster

Bill Evo, Former President of the Detroit Red Wings, former professional hockey player

ENTREPRENEURS
Jerry Levin, CEO, Time Warner

Larry Rosenfeld and Rick Flax, Co-Founders, the California Pizza Kitchen

Anne Martin, Senior Sales Director, Mary Kay Cosmetics

Tim and Nina Zagat, Publisher of Zagat's restaurant and hotel guides

ARTISTS
Otto Preminger, Filmaker

Bernard Jacobs, President of the Shubert Organization

Cole Porter, Musician

Paul Cezanne, Artist

Igor Stravinsky, Musician

POLITICAL LEADERS
Bill Clinton, President

Mahatma Gandhi, Political Leader, India

Resources

RECOMMENDED RESOURCES

American Bar Association, Breaking Traditions: Work Alternatives for Lawyers, American Bar Association, Chicago, IL (1993).

American Bar Association, Changing Jobs: A Handbook for Lawyers for the 1990s, American Bar Association, Chicago, IL (1994).

American Bar Association and Peterson's, Full Disclosure: Do You Really Want to Be a Lawyer?, American Bar Association and Peterson's, Chicago, IL (1992).

Anderson, Nancy, Work With Passion, Carol & Graff and Whatever Publishing (1984).

Arron, Deborah, Running From the Law: Why Good Lawyers Are Getting Out of the Legal Profession, Niche Press, Seattle, WA (1992).

Arron, Deborah and Guyol, The Complete Guide to Contract Lawyering: What Every Lawyer and Law Firm Needs to Know about Temporary Legal Services, Niche Press, Seattle, WA (1992).

Bell, Susan, Full Disclosure: Do You Really Want to Be a Lawyer?, American Bar Association, Young Lawyers Decision (1989).

Bolles, Richard N., What Color is your Parachute? A Practical Manual for Job-Hunters and Career Changers, Ten Speed Press, Berkeley, CA (1997).

Bolles, Richard N., The Three Boxes of Life (And How to Get Out of Them), Ten Speed Press, Berkeley, CA (1981).

Brady, Kathleen, What Lawyers Earn, HarcourtBrace, 1997.

Bridges, William, Transitions: Making Sense of Life's Changes, Addison-Wesley (1988).

Byers, Mark, Don Samuelson, Gordon Williamson, Lawyers in Transition: Planning a Life in the Law, The Barkley Company, Natick, MA (1988).

Cain, Turning Points, American Bar Association, Chicago, IL (1994).

Chin-Lee, Cynthia, It's Who You Know - Career Strategies for Making Effective Personal Contacts, Pfeiffer and Co. (1993).

Federal Reports, Directory of Graduate Law Degree Programs, Federal Reports, Washington, DC (1993).

Federal Reports, Federal Law Related Careers: A Guide to Over 80 Law-Related Careers, Federal Reports, Washington, DC (1987).

Figler, Howard and Henry Holt, The Complete Job-Search Handbook (1988).

Fruedenberger, Herbert J., M.D., Burn Out: How to Beat the High Cost of Success, Bantam Books (1980).

Grant and Werner, The Road Not Taken, National Association of Law Placement (1991).

Grant and Werner, The Road Not Taken - Job Seeker Excerpts, National Association of Law Placement (1991).

Jackson, Tom, Guerrilla Tactics in the New Job Market, Bantam Books, New York, NY (1991).

Kantor, The Essential Book of Interviewing, Random House (1995).

Law School Admission Council, The Official Guide to U.S. Law Schools, Law School Admission Council (1996).

Mantis, Hillary J. and Kathleen Brady, Jobs for Lawyers: Effective Techniques for Getting Hired in Today's Marketplace, Impact Publications, Manassas Park, VA (1996).

Medley, Sweaty Palms: The Neglected Art of Being Interviewed (1992).

Moll, Richard W., The Lure of the Law: Why People Become Lawyers and What the Profession Does to Them, Viking Penguin, New York, NY (1990).

Noble, Bob, The Job Search Handbook: Basics of a Professional Job Search, Bob Adams, Inc. (1988).

Patent, Arnold, You Can Have It All: The Art of Winning the Money Game and Living a Life of Joy, Celebration Publishing (1988).

Sher, Barbara, Wishcraft: How to Get What You Really Want, Ballentine Books, New York, NY (1979).

Simon, Sydney B., M.D., Getting Unstuck: Breaking Through the Barriers to Change, Warner Books (1988).
Sinetar, Marsha, Do What You Love, The Money Will Follow, Paulist Press New York, NY (1987).

Stoodley, Information Interviewing: What It Is and How to Use It in Your Career (1990).

Utley, Frances, Non-Legal Careers for Lawyers in the Private Sector, American Bar Association, Chicago, IL (1984).

Walton, Kimm Alayne, Guerilla Tactics for Getting the Legal Job of Your Dreams, HarcourtBrace (1996).

Wilson Schaef, Anne and Diane Fassel, The Addictive Organization, Harper & Row (1988).

APPENDIX

PRO BONO OPPORTUNITIES—
ASSOCIATION OF THE BAR OF THE
CITY OF NEW YORK

(adapted from "Pro Bono Opportunities," published by the Association of the Bar of the City of New York, 1995 edition)

ADVOCATES FOR CHILDREN OF NEW YORK (AFC).

Advocates for students who encounter problems with the NYC public school system.

Qualifications/Requirements:

Training is conducted by AFC on the procedures associated with administrative hearings and is mandatory prior to taking a case. Volunteers are provided with manuals and other written materials and are given continuing support by AFC attorneys and staff. Spanish language skills useful.

AIDS CENTER OF QUEENS COUNTY, INC. (ACQC)

Provides comprehensive social services for people with HIV/AIDS in Queens- wills, estate planning, gov't benefits, insurance, bankruptcy, immigration, landlord/tenant, consumer/debt.

Qualifications/ Requirements:

All volunteers must attend a general orientation. Wills clinic training available. Spanish or Haitian Creole language skills useful.

AMERICAN CIVIL LIBERTIES UNION. (ACLU)

Concentrates on efforts preserve constitutional freedoms, challenges civil rights violations and efforts to expand Bill of Rights protection for the individual.

Qualifications/Requirements:

None listed.

AMERICAN INDIAN LAW ALLIANCE (AILA)

Provides legal services, information and advice to Native American clients.

Qualifications/Requirements:

Admitted to bar; in practice for over six months, a good understanding of the law. Cultural training workshops available.

ASIAN AMERICAN LEGAL DEFENSE AND EDUCATION FUND (AALDEF)

Impact litigation and community education in the areas of voting rights, immigrants' rights, anti-Asian violence, employment rights, environmental justice and Japanese-American redress.

Qualifications/Requirements:

None listed.

ASSOCIATION FOR UNION DEMOCRACY

Promotes the principles and practices of internal union democracy in the American labor movement.

Qualifications/Requirements:

Landrum-Griffin Act expertise is useful, not necessary.

THE BETTER BUSINESS BUREAU OF METROPOLITAN NEW YORK (BBB)

Provides pre-purchase information; mediation and arbitration for consumer complaints; investigates misleading and deceptive advertising and selling practices

Qualifications/Requirements:

Must attend a two-evening training session. Mediation training provided.

CARDOZO BET TZEDEK LEGAL SERVICES

Provides representation in civil cases to elderly and disabled individuals unable to afford private counsel. Wills, government benefits and consumer cases.

Qualifications/Requirements:

None listed. Yiddish, Russian language skills useful.

CENTER FOR IMMIGRATION RIGHTS, INC. (CIR)

Counsels immigrants with problems of immigration, employment abuse and discrimination, wage and hours standards, workplace safety, HIV waivers, access to health and public benefits, city/state services, and other poverty law issues.

Qualifications/Requirements:

The legal director and CIR staff provide orientation and backup. Fluency in Spanish, Creole, Chinese, Russian, and other languages useful.

COALITION FOR THE HOMELESS

Dedicated to principle that decent shelter, adequate food supply and affordable housing are fundamental rights.

Qualifications/Requirements:

None listed.

COVENANT HOUSE LEGAL DEPARTMENT

Represents runaway and homeless youths on a variety of legal issues.

Qualifications/Requirements:

None listed. Spanish language skills useful.

THE DOOR-A CENTER OF ALTERNATIVES

Provides legal advocacy for children between 12 and 21, including mental health, education, creative and physical arts, and legal advocacy.

Qualifications/Requirements:

None listed. Lawyers with experience in immigration, housing, family law, and public benefits especially needed. Fluency in Spanish useful.

EASTSIDE IMPROVEMENT SOCIETY, INC.

Provides legal assistance on housing issues including landlord/tenant, family law, negligence, bankruptcy, trusts and estates, coop and condo law, and pensions.

Qualifications/ Requirements:

Lawyers need at least two years of experience. Spanish language skills useful.

GAY MEN'S HEALTH CRISIS, INC.

Legal Services Department

PROVIDES LEGAL SERVICES TO PERSONS WITH AIDS AND SYMPTOMATIC HIV. LAW COVERED:

wills, power of attorney, advanced medical directives, immigration, landlord/tenant, debtor/creditor, confidentiality, insurance, discrimination and family law matters.

Qualifications/ Requirements:

None listed.

HIV LAW PROJECT

Provides legal representation and advocacy to low income, HIV positive individuals. Law covered: discrimination, land-lord/tenant, denial of financial entitlement, custody, healthcare, living wills, power of attorney, class action lawsuits, remedial legislation.

Qualifications/ Requirements:

None listed.

JEWISH BOARD OF FAMILY AND CHILDREN'S SERVICES

The Jewish Conciliation Board of America (JCBA)
Provides mediation/conciliation and arbitration services, (provides own arbitration panels, etc.)

Qualifications/ Requirements:

Knowledge of Jewish law, Yiddish, Hebrew or Russian language skills useful.

JEWISH COMMUNITY RELATIONS COUNCIL

Jewish Legal Assistance
Provides legal assistance to Jewish communal and religious organizations.

Qualifications/ Requirements:

Volunteers need for litigation and non-profit corporate, real estate and tax matters.

LAMBDA LEGAL DEFENSE AND EDUCATION FUND, INC.

Brings test case litigation and provides education on civil rights on behalf of gays and lesbians and those with AIDS. Law covered: constitutional law, discrimination, civil rights, family law, housing, employment law, and HIV/AIDS. Lambda also does advocacy on health care reform, and confidentiality/disclosure and testing issues.

Qualifications/ Requirements:

Non-listed. Non-coastal (Heartland) volunteers particularly needed.

LAWYERS ALLIANCE FOR NEW YORK

Provides legal services to not-for-profit organizations concerned with improving housing, education, jobs, transportation and social welfare for low-income New Yorkers.

Qualifications/ Requirements:
Training provided. Spanish language skills useful.

LAWYERS COMMITTEE FOR HUMAN RIGHTS

Promotes respect for and observance of international human rights and refugee law. Volunteers litigate individual asylum cases.

Qualifications/ Requirements:
No experience necessary. Training provided. Foreign language fluency useful.

LAWYERS FOR CHILDREN, INC.

Represents children who have been voluntarily placed in foster care by their parents, educates children of their legal rights.

Qualifications/ Requirements:
Training available to volunteers who give 20+ hours per week. Volunteers needed for writing amicus briefs, doing research.

LEGAL ACTION CENTER FOR THE HOMELESS

Provides legal services to the homeless and near-homeless.

Qualifications/ Requirements:
None listed. Training provided.

LEGAL ACTION CENTER OF THE CITY OF NEW YORK

Performs test-case litigation and provides legal services to recovering drug and alcohol abusers, ex-offenders and people with AIDS in discrimination matters.

Qualifications/ Requirements:
Volunteers needed to work on discrimination matters and AIDS-related family, housing and healthcare issues.

THE LEGAL AID SOCIETY; VOLUNTEER DIVISION/ COMMUNITY LAW OFFICES

Provides comprehensive legal services in landlord/tenant, matrimonial, family law, consumer matters, corporate matters, community development, Article 78 proceedings, appeals, impact legislation, and administrative proceedings. Projects in neighborhood offices focus on the elderly, persons with AIDS, homeless families, immigrants, battered spouses, the disabled, and community-based organizations.

Qualifications/ Requirements:

None listed. Training provided.

Neighborhood offices:

Bronx, Brooklyn, Chelsea, Rockaway, Queens, Harlem, Staten Island

LEGAL SERVICES FOR NEW YORK CITY (LSNY)

Provides representation in civil matters to poor persons in such areas as housing, family, consumer and health issues.

Qualifications/ Requirements:

Assistance particularly needed in areas of bankrupcy, consumer, discrimination, employment, family, government benefits, housing, matrimonial, and wills. Training available.

Neighborhood Offices:

Various offices in Bronx, Brooklyn, Manhattan, and Queens

THE LESBIAN AND GAY LAW ASSOCIATION OF GREATER NEW YORK

Provides a walk-in clinic. Cannot provide direct representation at this time.

Qualifications/ Requirements:

None listed.

NAACP LEGAL DEFENSE AND EDUCATION FUND, INC.

Provides litigation services in employment and housing discrimination, health care, school desegregation, police miscon-
duct, capital punishment and other civil rights matters.

Qualifications/ Requirements:

Training available. Volunteers particularly needed in areas of
certiorari petitions, post-conviction and habeas corpus proceedings in capital punishment cases, and employment discrimination.

NATIONAL CENTER ON WOMEN & FAMILY LAW

Provides legal assistance on family law issues to low-income
women.

Qualifications/ Requirements:

Training available.

NETWORK FOR WOMEN'S SERVICES

Provides legal services to indigent women: family law service
to victims of domestic violence; family law issues and living
wills and health care proxies to HIV+ women; and immigration assistance for immigrant battered women.

Qualifications/ Requirements:

None listed. Spanish or other foreign language skills useful.

NEW YORK ASSOCIATION FOR NEW AMERICANS, INC. (NYANA)

Assists individuals with immigration-related matters. Volunteers represent individuals in preparing and filing applications
with the INS.

Qualifications/ Requirements:

No prior experience necessary. Training provided.

NEW YORK LAWYERS FOR THE PUBLIC INTEREST, INC. (NYLPI)

Provides public interest legal assistance. Particular focus on
health, mental health, developmental disabilities, and land use
law.

Qualifications/ Requirements:

None listed.

NEW YORK LEGAL ASSISTANCE GROUP. INC.

Provides legal services on a broad range of issues affecting low-income people, except for housing, including government benefits, matrimonial/family law, and wills matters.

Qualifications/ Requirements:

Volunteers must make a 6 month minimum commitment of at least 20 hours per week spread over three days in the office. Fluency in Russian, Spanish, Haitian Creole, and American Sign Language useful.

NORTHERN MANHATTAN IMPROVEMENT CORPORATION

Provides free housing legal services to community resident of Washington Heights-Inwood and Marble Hill.

Qualifications/ Requirements:

None listed. Spanish, Greek or Russian language skills useful. Volunteers with some familiarity of rent control and rent stabilization, as well as housing and summary proceedings particularly needed.

NOW LEGAL DEFENSE AND EDUCATION FUND

Provides legal assistance with the goal of securing equality of rights under law for women.

Qualifications/ Requirements:

Volunteers with experience in employment discrimination, reproductive rights, welfare matters, constitutional law and civil rights desirable. Training available.

PHOENIX HOUSE FOUNDATION, INC.

Provides legal assistance to drug-rehabilitation center residents.

Qualifications/ Requirements:

Volunteers with experience in the areas of family law, consumer, employment, tax and veterans benefits needed. Training provided.

PRISONERS' LEGAL SERVICES OF NEW YORK

Provides legal services to indigent prisoners in NY state correctional facilities, particularly in Article 78 proceedings, challenging disciplinary hearing decisions, civil rights actions, and visitation and custody cases.

Qualifications/ Requirements:

Training provided. Spanish language skills useful.

PUERTO RICAN LEGAL DEFENSE AND EDUCATION FUND

Provides legal assistance with goal of protecting civil rights and liberties of Latinos. Areas of law include voter participation, housing, education and employment.

Qualifications/ Requirements:

Lawyers with experience in civil rights, employment, education, family law, housing, language rights and voting rights needed. All volunteers must attend a general orientation.

SANCTUARY FOR FAMILIES, INC.

Center for Battered Women's Legal Services
Provides legal representation for battered women in family court and matrimonial matters and in some criminal cases.

Qualifications/ Requirements:

Training provided.

VICTIM SERVICES

Provides legal assistance to crime victims and their families in order to reduce psychological, physical and financial hardships they suffer.

Qualifications/Requirements:

None listed.

VICTIM SERVICES—TRAVELERS AID IMMIGRATION LEGAL SERVICES

Provides counsel to immigrants on obtaining legal status.

Qualifications/ Requirements:

Experience in immigration law and fluency in one or more foreign languages preferred. Training available.

VICTIM SERVICES—WESTSIDE OFFICE LEGAL PROJECT

Represents domestic violence victims in matrimonial, family offense, custody, and visitation cases.

Qualifications/Requirements:

Training provided.

VOLUNTEER LAWYERS FOR THE ARTS, INC. (VLA)

Provides free legal assistance to income-eligible artists and arts organizations with arts-related legal problems. Areas of law include copyright, contract, immigration, insurance, and litigation matters.

Qualifications/Requirements:

Lawyers must be admitted to NY State Bar and must attend an orientation session.

VOLUNTEERS OF LEGAL SERVICE (VOLS)

Provides frcc civil legal services to poor persons living in New York City by matching cases to law firms and corporate law departments.

Qualifications/Requirements:

Firms that will commit 30 hours of pro bono work per attorney per year are preferred, but not required.

WEST SIDE SRO LAW PROJECT GODDARD—RIVERSIDE COMMUNITY CENTER

Provides legal services to individuals and groups of indigent single adults living in Single Room Occupancy (SRO) buildings on the West Side in matters relating to tenancy.

Qualifications/ Requirements:

None listed.

YOUTH ADVOCACY CENTER, INC.

Tries to introduce the voice of foster care youth to the public dialogue about child welfare policy and practice. Specific issues include education rights of foster children and the rights of pregnant and parenting teens in foster care.

Qualifications/ Requirements:
Training available.

PRO BONO OPPORTUNITIES:

Court and Government Programs

Bronx County Supreme Court, Civil Branch

Civil Court of the City of New York

Small Claims Arbitrators

Court Appointed Special Advocates

New York City Commission on Human Rights

Pro Bono Assistance Program

New York State Division on Human Rights

Queens County District Attorney's Office

Appeals Bureau Pro Bono Program

United States Court of Appeals for the Second Circuit

Pro Bono Panel

United States District Court for the Eastern District of New York

Civil Pro Bono Panel

United States District Court for the Southern District of New York

Pro Bono Panel

ABOUT THE AUTHOR

Hillary J. Mantis, Esq., is Director of the Career Planning Center at Fordham University School of Law, a career management expert for attorneys and law students, and an author. Ms. Mantis has appeared on television and radio shows as a career expert and has spoken and conducted many programs at Fordham University Law School, New York Law School, the New York City Bar Association, the New York County Lawyers' Association and the American Bar Association. She is the co-author of *Jobs For Lawyers, Effective Techniques for Getting Hired in Today's Legal Marketplace* (Impact Publications, 1996).

Ms. Mantis served as Chair of the American Bar Association Young Lawyers Division Career Issues Committee in 1993–94. In addition, she was Chair of the New York County Lawyers' Association Committee on Lawyer Placement, Subcommittee Chair of the Association of the Bar of the City of New York's special Committee on Law Student Perspectives, and served as the National Association for Law Placement's Liaison to the A.B.A. Section on Law Practice Management. She was on the editorial board of the American Bar Association's Barrister Magazine from 1994–1995.

She has also published several articles on career development in publications including *The New York Law Journal* and the *National Association for Law Placement Annual Review.*

She has written a chapter in *Breaking Traditions: Work Alternatives for Lawyers,* published by the Law Practice Management Section of the A.B.A., and has written a chapter and served as contributing editor of *Changing Jobs: A Handbook for Lawyers in the '90s,* published by the A.B.A. Young

Lawyers Division. Ms. Mantis developed and wrote a regular career column, *Career Notes*, for the New York County Lawyer's Association Bulletin for three years.

Prior to joining the staff of Fordham, she was Associate Director of Career Services at New York Law School. She is a graduate of Brown University and Boston College Law School. Her recruitment and counseling activities have included specialized work in the areas of alternative legal careers, public interest employment and alumni career counseling.

Prior to joining the staff of New York Law School, she was involved in politics and public interest law.

If you would like to contact the author, you may reach her at: careers@mail.lawnet.fordham.edu

NOTES

NOTES

NOTES

NOTES

NOTES

NOTES

WHAT AM I GOING TO DO?

We can help you answer that question, whether you're just getting out of college, have a graduate degree, or simply want to change your career path.